CHILDREN, these are MY WORDS

In The School of Hard Knocks

Jerry and Virginia Kasha
and Merle (Mo) Hogan

Copyright © 2014 by Jerry and Virginia Kasha and Merle(Mo)Hogan

"Children, these are My Words"
In The School of Hard Knocks
by Jerry and Virginia Kasha and Merle(Mo)Hogan

Printed in the United States of America

Edited by Xulon Press

ISBN 9781498411271

All rights reserved solely by the author. The author guarantees all contents are original and do not infringe upon the legal rights of any other person or work. No part of this book may be reproduced in any form without the permission of the author. The views expressed in this book are not necessarily those of the publisher.

Scripture quotations taken from the New International Version (NIV). Copyright © 1973, 1978, 1984, 2011 by Biblica, Inc.™. Used by permission. All rights reserved.

Scripture quotations taken from the New King James Version (NKJV). Copyright © 1979, 1980, 1982 by Thomas Nelson, Inc. Used by permission. All rights reserved.

Scripture quotations taken from the New Living Translation (NLT). Copyright © 1996, 2004, 2007 by Tyndale House Foundation. Used by permission. All rights reserved.

Scripture quotations taken from the New American Standard Bible (NASB). Copyright © 1960, 1962, 1963, 1968, 1971, 1972, 1973, 1975, 1977, 1995 by The Lockman Foundation. Used by permission. All rights reserved.

www.xulonpress.com

TABLE OF CONTENTS

Dedication vii

<u>Assignments</u>
   1.   The Beginning. 9
   2.   Heading Off Track 21
   3.   Learning to Temper Our Tongues . . 37
   4.   Were We Like Jonah?. 45
   5.   "Come To Me First" 59
   6.   How Much He Loves Us. 71
   7.   Why Did We Worry?. 99
   8.   Speaking To One A Day. 125
   9.   Identifying With the Prophets 139
  10.   Procrastination to Disobedience . . 159
  11.   Alone In The Boat 171
  12.   God's Timeline 205
  13.   "I AM" 223
  14.   "Today and Forever" 245

Testimonies 285
Finally Brothers and Sisters 291

v

DEDICATION

To our Heavenly, Faithful God, Yeshua, Jesus Christ our Lord. You are Omnipresent, Omnipotent and our One True God.

From the second we were conceived in our mothers' wombs, You have watched over our every breath. You know our intimate thoughts, and what is in our hearts, minds, and souls. We have the assurance that You will never leave us.

You continually gave us comfort, strength and compassion when we strayed. Lord, we thank You for Your unconditional love, and for staying with us throughout this journey.

Thank You! We love You, Lord!
You are the great "I AM."

ASSIGNMENT 1

THE BEGINNING

BUILDING

These men called together their fellow Levites, and they all purified themselves. Then they began to cleanse the temple of the Lord, just as the king had commanded. They were careful to follow all the Lord's instructions in their work.
2 Chronicles 29:15 (NLT)

THE BEGINNING

God has now revealed to us his mysterious plan regarding Christ, a plan to fulfill his own good pleasure. And this is the plan: At the right time he will bring everything together under the authority of Christ – everything in heaven and on earth. Furthermore, because we are united with Christ, we have received an inheritance from God, for he chose us in advance, and he makes everything work out according to his plan.
Ephesians 1:9-11 (NLT)

Do you remember your first day in a new classroom? Was there a sense of anxiety, excitement, confusion and fear of beginning something new? Those were the feelings the three of us experienced as we launched out on a journey through the hallways of the "School of Hard Knocks." You were assigned a "home room," where you sat and waited for the individual in charge, your teacher, to explain what was to come. On our first day in this new classroom, our teacher, the Lord, explained to us what was to come our way through His school. He would only reveal one assignment at a time. We were not to go to the next class until we had finished the task He had given us. Even if the bell rang, we were to stay to finish our test. He said He would guide us, help us, encourage us, and be with us until we graduated. That was encouraging, but He also advised us that we would be disciplined if we decided to do things our way and not follow His rules. Having received the rules and guidelines for this walk through the hallways of the "School of Hard Knocks," we were anxious to leave our "home room" and get started on our journey. We could hardly contain our enthusiasm and excitement as we entered the hallway to go to our first class with the Lord.

Prior to starting this journey, God, in His infinite wisdom, had placed Jerry, Virginia and Merle together, serving the Lord, several years earlier. God's intent was for these three children to hear His words. In order to learn to trust each other and rely solely on the Lord, He sent them into the mission field together. Little did they know that learning to hear His words would be the beginning in the "School of Hard Knocks."

Who would have thought that while browsing through a bookstore, Jerry's life and that of two others would be forever changed? Walking down one

The Beginning

of the aisles, a book about spiritual housecleaning caught his attention. After casually glancing through the book, it was placed back on the shelf. Later that day, while driving home, Jerry sensed the Holy Spirit saying, **"There is a building that needs gentle, prayerful, spiritual healing."** His first thought was, "*You have to be kidding.*" The overwhelming sense of peace that settled on his spirit was so comforting and convincing that all he could say was, "Okay!"

Realizing that he didn't know what this entailed, nor if he could accomplish this alone, Jerry asked the Lord who He would send to help him. He replied, **"Your wife, Virginia, and Merle Hogan (Mo)."** Mo is a Messianic Jewish friend and prayer partner, whom we have known for several years. After speaking with Virginia, a call to Mo was placed to ask if she would be willing to be involved with this assignment. The three of us then went into prayer concerning the words that Jerry had heard.

What if you were asked to go on a journey to a place that you have never been before? The time frame had no specific ending and you were told there were two other people going on the journey with you. Perhaps your reaction would reflect thoughts of, "I'm not sure about that. More details are needed. The unknown could be fun." Then, the concerns would surface. Who are these other two people, and do we know if we would like each other? Why would we agree to go, not knowing when the journey would end? Would we be able to do what was asked the way it was told? Would we try to make our own path, instead of trusting the words of the Lord? Much prayer and listening was needed. Knowing we could do all things through Christ, we sensed that He would equip us, as long as the three of us prayed and kept our focus on the Lord.

God was tugging on our "heart strings" and we knew that this pull was something different than anything we had ever experienced. We couldn't even explain our inner thoughts to each other at this time. That pull, still buried deep within our spirit, dictated we had to explore our feelings further. All we knew, when we talked about it, was that it was uncharted territory that intrigued each of us. Because we did not yet understand the spiritual depth and commitment that it would take to accomplish such a task, we were uncomfortable with our human understanding of this new venture. What was this "God Journey" that He was asking us to take? Just that statement alone threw us into a state of confusion for answers. Did we really comprehend what God was asking of us? We didn't have a clue how the three of us were going to go about this assignment. More questions popped into our minds. Why were the three of us, with different

The Beginning

religious backgrounds, chosen to be together on this journey? Could we make this commitment to the Lord? Would we have strength enough to be obedient? Were we ready to take this leap of faith? Would we recognize His voice when He spoke to us?

After much prayer and many more thoughts and concerns, we became comfortable with the fact that if God brought us to this place, He would take us through to completion. We had also adjusted to the fact that if we said "Yes" to this journey, the three of us were going to be "joined at the hip" for such a time as this.

The Lord revealed to Jerry what He specifically wanted him to do to prepare for this assignment. He said, **"Fast on Sunday."** "But Lord, that is Easter Sunday and the entire family will be at our house for dinner." Again The Lord said, **"I want you to fast on Sunday."** Many reading this book may say that it is not proper to fast on a religious holiday, *but if the Lord says to do it, DO IT.*

After hearing His words, Jerry went to a local coffee house, ordered a cup of tea and sat outside at one of the patio tables. With his eyes closed, he asked the Lord to let him enter into His presence. At this point many people will ask, "How does one enter into His intimate presence?" That question would have to be answered by each individual. For Jerry, he simply closes his eyes and asks the Lord to bring him the peace that only He can provide. Asking to enter into His presence, the Lord spoke and said, **"Jerry, open your eyes! I made all that you see. You are always in My presence, you just don't realize it."** It was hard to believe that the Lord actually spoke to him. There was such a sense of amazement that God would choose an average person to do something for Him. After pondering that thought, Jerry was prompted by the Lord to consider, "Why not? I am His child, a member of His family." It was an awe-inspiring and humbling sensation to have had a conversation with the Lord. A friend of mine asked me, "How do you have a conversation with the Lord?" My response was, "Simply ask, 'Lord, can we talk?'" Sometimes He answers and we talk, and other times He chooses to remain silent. Again, that question of having a conversation with the Lord must be answered by each individual.

During Jerry's quiet time to pray, the Lord revealed to him that he should walk around the designated building one time, going from east to west. While walking, Jerry was to pray and then remove any negative barriers from that building (meaning to cast out/remove the weaker, disruptive spirits) by declaring the words of the Lord, **"In the Name of Jesus, be removed."** The Lord continued by saying, **"Do not be afraid for I, The Lord, have conquered the world. By the power of Jesus' name, make a dent in Satan's armor."** If you take out the army privates and corporals, the captains have less of an army with which to fight. The Lord said, **"When you depart say, 'Let the living waters of the Spirit of Christ flow through this building.'"**

During that conversation, Jerry was told that there were more of us, (meaning that the Lord had provided His angels to accompany us on this task) than there were of them (disruptive spirits). The Lord reminded Jerry of the story about Elisha and his servant.

> *When the servant of the man of God got up and went out early the next morning, an army with horses and chariots had surrounded the city. "Oh, my Lord, what shall we do?" the servant asked. "Don't be afraid," the prophet answered. "Those who are with us are more than those who are with them." And Elisha prayed, "O Lord, open his eyes so he may see." Then the Lord opened the servant's eyes and he looked and saw the hills full of horses and chariots of fire all around Elisha.*
> 2 Kings 6:15-17 (NIV)

Again, this triggered Jerry's memory of the story of Gideon and his fight. Gideon had thousands of troops ready to fight the enemy, but the Lord reduced his ranks two times, by the thousands. Gideon was left with only three hundred men, which he then broke into three squads of 100 men each, and defeated the enemy.

On the day that we went to pray, the three of us met for prayer prior to going to the building. We asked the Lord for guidance and discernment, as well as for protection. Arriving at the specified building, Jerry walked around it, praying, as instructed. The Lord instructed Merle and Virginia to symbolically hold up Jerry's arms.

> *As long as Moses held up his hands, the Israelites were winning, but whenever he lowered his hands, the Amalekites were winning. When Moses' hands grew tired, they took a stone and put it under him and he sat on it. Aaron and Hur held his hands up – one on one side, one on the other – so that his hands remained steady till sunset. So Joshua overcame the Amalekite army with the sword. Exodus 17:11-13 (NIV)*

Prior to entering the building, we prayed for encouragement, strength, and the ability to focus on what He wanted us to do. The Lord was very specific about us listening and not trying to second guess what should be done next. He advised us that He would give us clear instructions about the order in which we were to move from room to room, and those things for which we were to pray. We then proceeded, as directed, praying and declaring God's blessings and peace in each room. Upon leaving, we gave thankful praises to the Lord for allowing us to be His vessels.

After completing our task, the Lord's instructions to us were to say:

"Let the living waters of the Spirit of Christ flow through this building."

Little did the three of us know that we were about to embark on the most incredible, thought-provoking, exciting, spiritual journey of our lives.

THE IMPORTANT THING IS NOT SO MUCH
WHERE WE STAND AS THE DIRECTION
IN WHICH WE ARE GOING

ASSIGNMENT 2

HEADING OFF TRACK

ROTTEN FRUIT TREE

Every tree that does not bear fruit will be cut down and thrown into the fire... Matthew 3:10 (NIV)

HEADING OFF TRACK

When I think of all of this, I fall to my knees and pray to the Father, the Creator of everything in heaven and on earth. I pray that from his glorious, unlimited resources he will empower you with inner strength through his Spirit. Then Christ will make his home in your hearts as you trust in him. Your roots will grow down into God's love and keep you strong. And may you have the power to understand, as all God's people should, how wide, how long, how high and how deep his love is. May you experience the love of Christ, though it is too great to understand fully. Then you will be made complete with all the fullness of life and power that comes from God.
Ephesians 3:14-19 (NLT)

From the very beginning, we learned we would hear, be taught, and guided by the Lord each step of the way. At first we had no idea what that meant. We kept listening very closely so we wouldn't miss His voice. Upon receiving His words, we were amazed at what we heard. For the next four days we prayed for many families/individuals while receiving words, visions and directions.

July 20 – **"My children, these are My words"**

"Power, Strength, Victory. My children, this prayer time I have set aside for you will not only be a healing for others, but it is to teach you how to pray deeper. You have prayed as I have asked, and have completed the tasks I have given you in the past. Now, as you pray, I need you to learn how to pray with power, strength and victory. I don't want your words and prayers to be casual. Attitudes must change so that walls will come down, and the victory will be Mine. Pray with a heart of Mine, loving, but with strength, and there will be victory through your prayers.

"As you pray and wish blessings for others, also pray and command them to be for you also. I am in charge. I need things to change now. Time is getting shorter. Don't worry or fret about the small things in the lives of others or yourselves. Stick to the hard-core issues. Things also have to change now for the three of you. Don't worry about the human side of things that will get in the way of your praying. Pray and ask Me for the godly things, and I will take care of the rest.

"My children, I need you to be strong with power and might. Don't worry about things getting better or worse in the times to come. Pray and know I have changed them. Don't look back on the others you have prayed for, and wonder if their lives have changed. When you have prayed for the families and you have accepted the prayers, know that whatever happens is up to Me. Go on with boldness, strength, power, and victory. Don't worry about 'IF,' know 'IT IS.'

"Your prayers have to be what I need them to be. Listen to whatever I want you to pray for others, even if it is not what you expect. Go and do your jobs. Pray for others, as well as yourselves. I can't wait for you to wonder if it is good or not. Do it, say it, anoint it, and go on, believing it is done.

"I need the three of you to be stronger. You may experience the same things that happened in Bible stories you have read. Behind each story there were set reasons and meanings. Recognize the difference between the good and bad. When you get stories, and dreams, you will also get interpretations. These are from Me! Listen, read, and act on them. You will get more of these, and I need you to continue with them.

"I am here for you and I will never leave you. Don't be afraid. You will pray, speak, feel, and see results differently. Don't be amazed, be glad, and be ready. I am waiting for you three to take the next step. Are you ready? I know you will do as I ask. Now is the time. I will get you prepared, starting tonight. You will see, feel, and know the difference in each other, because you will all be the same. Now get up and get going. March down the straight and narrow path. You are ready, and have shown you are ready. Before your prayers dry up, listen to Me and act. Now be strong, in power, and with victory. I am the Lord your God and will take you where I need you to go. My blessings and love are with you now and always."

Your Heavenly Father, God.

The message we received was very clear. We knew beyond a shadow of a doubt that we were only the messengers. God was calling us to take part in making His message known. The Lord wanted us to experience His unconditional love for us so that we, in turn, could pray for others with a deeper conviction. We knew there would be those who would not be convinced that God still speaks to His children. He wanted us to learn about the goodness of others, and bless them where they were in their walk with the Lord. It was a time of conviction for us. The three of us were still learning to move forward with a positive attitude, knowing that God is, and always will be, in control of every situation. The words we received from the Lord stated that He couldn't wait for us to decide whether things were good or bad. He was asking us to pray about it, anoint it (meaning that our prayers were blessed by God), and go on, believing that it was done. The reality is that He wants to be number one in our lives on a daily basis. The Lord was asking us to make a conscious effort to commit to a deeper relationship with Him and pray from our hearts. That meant humbly acknowledging and prayerfully thanking Him for every situation, whether it was positive or negative. He did not want us to lose our enthusiasm to focus, pray and glorify Him seven days a week.

July 21–**"My children, these are My words"**
"Do you know how proud I am of you three, learning the goodness of others, and blessing the children I have set before you? Keep your eyes and ears opened. Be careful not to think all will be fun and games. There will be times you will be hit hard. When it hits home, be aware of My words you have learned. I will still take you deeper, and lift you up. You will continue with words, scriptures and visions. You are going to take a new direction. I need you to be stronger for the ones to come. They will have more detailed issues that will be harder to understand. It may be difficult because you don't understand their inner thoughts. If you ask, you will receive. I am here, you are there. I

know you want more and are excited, but don't get ahead of your senses. Listen, verbally praise My name, and sing praises to My name. We need to meet and get stronger. Now, let's take another journey together. You will walk down still another path. Stay strong, but humble. You are not to just be excited. Stay calm, and remember My name, God, Jesus, Holy Spirit."

We definitely were on a new path that looked different than anything we had experienced before. For the next two days we prayed positive and uplifting scriptures over many families. It was vital that we become more focused and listen with a new understanding of what the Lord wanted us to retain for the remainder of our journey.

July 23–"My children, these are My words"
"My children, do you know how proud I am of you? You have been passing My tests, listening to My words and obeying My commands. Now that you have proven yourselves faithful, your journey will begin and blossom. I had to test the three of you to see if you would obey and listen. Now that you have, you will go even deeper. You will pray, hear and read with much more clarity, devotion, and dedication.

"You have been set apart for such a time as this. Continue down My path. You are My treasures. Focus, hear and pray!

"I am here and you will start to see actual signs and wonders. It will be amazing to you. Just enjoy it and walk in My light. I have you surrounded with My covering.

"Turn loose. Go deeper. Listen, but not with fear of My being too stern. Why have you doubted? You are obedient, but are not completely assured of yourselves. Give all your cares to God. He will handle everything.

"Enjoy the journey, but be careful. Don't get full of yourselves. You three will go deeper on the journey. Bring My children back to Me 'stronger.' Be mindful of the words you speak, see, and hear. Let it be Me, Me, and Me.

"Thank you, children, thank you. You are saving souls and rescuing My children. Keep it going and watch for signs and wonders. They will be clear. Look for them, listen to them, and hold on to them. You three are ready. Today was a small step that will get larger and easier to accomplish. Walk, pray, laugh and obey! You are going to hear more, see more, and feel more. Now get some rest!" God

We were still learning that His ways are higher than ours, and struggled at times to find the words to gratefully thank the Lord for all that He was teaching us. Even though we knew we were beginners, this was such an exciting time for us. It became very apparent that we needed to listen and focus, because so much was happening in each of our lives. We were beginning to hear more, feel more, and see more. Our journey looked different to each of us, but we knew that we were walking down the same path. The Lord was teaching us to lean on the encouragement that He was giving us.

July 25 – **"My children, these are My words"**

"Why are My children so afraid to seek Me more? Why do they run from Me? I have given such love. Why do you think this happened? I need the three of you to spread the word about how much I really love them all. Search your hearts and feel the pain I have for My children. You will not carry this burden, but it will teach you how to pray with more boldness, assurance, and with love and dedication to Me.

"I will take you down My path, the path I walk with My Father. You will now learn about the love I have for all. I want you to guide others down that path, after you have learned to walk on it. Have patience in walking. Place one foot in front

of the other, feel My presence, and hear My voice. We will walk slowly and you will be set apart for such a time as this. Know when I call out to you. Be aware and get ready, your path will be narrow, but filled with wisdom. I am your teacher and you will learn.

"Walk, don't run! Tread softly and don't kick up the dirt. You need this path to guide you where you are directed to go. You will enjoy My words. Some scriptures I give will be for you to learn. Read them and learn from all of them. When you get scriptures, pray. They will either be for you, or those for whom you are praying. ALL SCRIPTURES HAVE MEANINGS!

"My path is set for your journey. Tomorrow will be another day. Rest tonight." God

During this time, we were three separate individuals walking on the same road. Each of us had a willingness and desire to serve the Lord. A passion to be obedient was beginning to stir within our spirits. However, the prayers and passions were individualized, as we struggled to learn how to bind our hearts together as one team walking the same road together. It was a learning curve for all three of us, and we sometimes settled for "second best" with our actions and reactions.

This "journey" concept was wonderful, but overwhelming to us at times. We struggled with the obedience and dedication to continually serve the Lord. It was hard for us to comprehend that the Lord had chosen the three of us to walk this road together. We found it difficult to discipline ourselves to be one unit, instead of three separate individuals. During our entire lives we had been programmed to think and act for ourselves. Now, the Lord was asking the three of us to think and act as one unit. Our conversations about how to do this became more frequent, more complicated, and less positive. We were dealing with three distinct personalities that didn't always blend into one unit. Knowing our confusion, the Lord began to show us, through visions, how we were settling for second best.

VISION 1: In the middle of a dry path there were three rocks, with a fruit tree growing in the center of the rocks. On the ground underneath the tree were many pieces of old, dried, and rotten fruit. At that specific time we were too lazy to climb up into the tree and reach for the beautiful, delicious, sun-ripened, fresh fruit at the top of the tree. Instead, we were picking up the rotten fruit on the ground, and settling for "second best."
INTERPRETATION: This vision showed us how lazy we were in reaching for the righteousness of the Lord. We thought we wanted something other than what we already had. We were definitely heading down a path of self-destruction. It was obvious that the discipline to stay focused was not on our radar screens. The Lord warned us that

we must rid ourselves of the rotten attitude that had become our daily lifestyle. Not only was it detrimental to our physical health, but it had become a major barrier to our spiritual growth.

VISION 2: There were two freight trains on the same track, traveling towards each other. Just before the trains were ready to collide, the Holy Spirit stepped in the middle of the track. The trains stopped before one was ready to go off the track. By stopping the trains, the Holy Spirit allowed one of the trains (representing us), to go forward to push the other train backward (which signified the enemy.)

INTERPRETATION: He warned us that we had come very close to submitting to the enemy and losing our power and strength to stay in God's will. The Holy Spirit, our Provider and Counselor, had spared us from yet another disaster. The Lord revealed to us that we must stay on the straight and narrow path, stand firm, and He would give us the strength and freedom to move forward. At this time, we were not focused, but the Lord assured us that He was walking with us and would never leave our side. We were still learning His ways.

There are numerous ways that visions are revealed by the Lord. A vision is a gift to you, from the Lord, and cannot be made up, or forced to happen. Sometimes the vision contains one scene. It happens quickly, remaining just long enough that you notice it, and then it vanishes. The picture is usually a one-screen snapshot, like a photo that does not have movement in it. Often the picture may come as a complete surprise, and is not a part of us or our mind. It is an experience that happens TO us and not THROUGH us. Another way is to see the vision in "the theatre of your mind." Instead of watching it on a real life movie screen, or television screen, you are seeing the vision in the form of a movie in your mind. It "floats" into your mind while the viewer is fully conscious and aware of his/her surroundings. It can happen when you have your eyes open, or when they are closed, perhaps in worship. Sometimes the Lord allows a person to see a bright light – like a "flash bulb" on a camera. The light places the focus on the exact spot that the vision may occur. This permits one to see and understand, with a conscious mind, the vision that the Lord wants the individual to remember. Visions can appear when in a deep rest and communing with the Lord. Some visions appear in color. The Lord often times gives the interpretation of visions immediately after the vision is seen. The meaning resonates deep in the "pit of the stomach," which leaves a peaceful sensation. Other times, the interpretation may come hours or days later. The Lord's timing is always perfect. He never makes mistakes with His delivery. We can only speak for ourselves, but some of you may identify with parts of these explanations. The Lord speaks to each individual in a way that they will comprehend what they have experienced.

You would have thought that after these two warnings we would have been jolted into reality. However, there would be many more lessons to be learned along the journey. We were definitely in the "School of Hard Knocks." Once again, we prayed together to ask for forgiveness and guidance. We knew and trusted the love of Jesus, the Hope of God, and the Movement of the Holy Spirit. Now, we just needed to actively apply those truths in our lives.

During this time, we had the honor and privilege of praying for many families and individuals. Instructions to the three of us were to pray for the same family, at the same time. The Lord told us, **"Do not judge! That is My job!"** Prayers of blessings, love and peace were lifted up to the Lord for each family/individual. Prayers included, but were not limited to: family, finances, health, relationships, jobs, spouses, children, property, etc. The time spent in prayer for others encouraged us to ask for those same blessings for ourselves. The more days we spent in prayer, the more focused and bolder we became on our mission. We learned to pray from our hearts, and be specific and to the point with our requests.

> THERE WAS A SENSE THAT WE WERE IN A PREPARATION PERIOD FOR DEEPER AND MORE INTIMATE ENCOUNTERS

ASSIGNMENT 3

LEARNING TO TEMPER OUR TONGUES

Friends/Family

Finally, all of you, live in harmony with one another, be sympathetic, love as brothers, be compassionate and humble. Do not repay evil with evil or insult with insult, but with blessing, because to this you were called so that you may inherit a blessing. 1 Peter 3:8-9 (NIV)

LEARNING TO TEMPER OUR TONGUES

For whoever would love life and see good days must keep his tongue from evil and his lips from deceitful speech. He must turn from evil and do good; he must seek peace and pursue it. For the eyes of the Lord are on the righteous and his ears are attentive to their prayer, but the face of the Lord is against those who do evil.
1 Peter 3:10-12 (NIV)

One of the first lessons we learned on the journey was about God's perfect timing. It became apparent to us very early in the journey that His timing looked completely different than what our human minds, with the concept of calendar days, could comprehend. Yes, we had agreed to go on a thirty-day journey. Comparing it to a calendar month, thirty days didn't seem too overwhelming in our minds. Oh, did we have a lot to learn! Who would have known that God's view of our first day into the journey would stretch out to be forty-four of our calendar days. Reality set in, and we knew that we had much more to learn about God's timing. During this time, we continued to read scriptures and pray blessings.

> But you must not forget this one thing, dear friends; A day is like a thousand years to the Lord, and a thousand years is like a day.
> 2 Peter 3:8 (NLT)

August 18–**"My children, these are My words"**

"The time has come. The time is right. You have walked many different paths, but you knew I was there at all times. You have done and heard well. You remained a team of love and devotion to one another. There was no shame, condemnation, nor wanting to be the one who heard the most. I love the way you were obedient. You were not afraid to speak of the visions. Your darkness was removed and you walked in My light. I treasure your hearts and how you handed them back to Me, because you learned that I COME FIRST in all things.

"Now you will all pray together and ask things to be done in My Name. There will be thirty days for a time to fast and pray healing prayers for the church. For these thirty days, you must fast from the tongue. There will be no negative words about family, friends, spouses or children, finances,

work place atmosphere, church, church members, music, or schedules. Pray a blessing over one person or family per day. Pronounce a different blessing on the church per day.

"At the end of thirty days, you will receive My words. For the next two days, pray for scriptures and blessings." AMEN

There was a sense of urgency that tugged at our hearts, to form a team of one; three cords woven together as one. Learning to be a team meant that we were prepared to work together with love, respect, and devotion to each other. It felt good to know we were striving to make those positive changes. As we listened to the Lord, we realized that He was instructing us how to walk in His light. He was reminding us that we must always put Him first, above all else. At first, our prayers were long and repetitious. We gradually learned to keep our words short, powerful, to the point, and always in His Name.

After receiving words for yet another journey, we questioned how we could possibly follow the guidelines placed before us. Each time we were given instructions, it was difficult to absorb, let alone accomplish. We wondered how we could be obedient enough to honor what the Lord had asked of us. Our human minds certainly didn't line up with the spiritual concept. With each new set of instructions, we were told that the Lord would sit with us, walk with us, talk with us, be our guide, and give us strength. It was hard to conceive that all of these promises from the Lord could be wrapped in one package. Yet, it sounded so simple. Our journey had already shown us that some of the days would be painful and the task set before us would be difficult. *But Lord, this time You told us to fast for thirty days.* We began to wonder what He had in mind regarding fasting. We soon learned the answer. The Lord specifically announced that we must fast from the tongue for thirty days. He was not making this a request — it was a command. He didn't want to hear one negative word from us about our workplace atmosphere, finances, spouses, or children, family, church, church members, music, schedules, and friends, for thirty days. All of a sudden, those thirty days seemed like a year. How do you keep what is in your mind from coming out of your mouth? Well, you probably have figured out by now how long that lasted. We managed to make it through most of the first day. The Lord was asking for our obedience to change unfitting, unbecoming, lifelong habits and learn to walk in His light. He knew ahead of time that we would be slow learners.

Little by little and day by day, our attitudes began to deteriorate. We began to question why we even agreed to take this thirty-day journey. It was getting harder and harder to think and stay positive. Following instructions, and silencing our negative words, soon became a thing of the past. Daily grumbling and complaining became an unattractive habit. We wondered if we had been overly enthusiastic about our decision to commit to this thirty-day walk. Was this ultimately going to benefit us in any way, shape or form? We still didn't understand, nor did we practice the concept of submission.

Does this story sound familiar? Was our scenario beginning to take shape and sound similar to the Old Testament Israelites? They, too, grumbled and complained as they wandered for forty years in the wilderness. We were wandering through our wilderness on a similar modernday journey. The Lord was only asking us to take a thirty-day journey. How hard could that be? When we said "yes" to the journey, it all sounded so simple.

The Lord instructed the three of us to spend the next two days researching Bible scriptures pertaining to blessings, and how we were not to be wise in our own eyes. As we investigated our Bible inquiry, two specific scriptures became blatant and very convicting:

> *Kind words are like honey, sweet to the soul and healthy for the body. Proverbs 16:24 (NLT)*
>
> *He who guards his mouth and his tongue keeps himself from calamity. Proverbs 21:23 (NIV)*

These scriptures caused us to examine our hearts and inner thoughts. If we looked in the mirror at ourselves, would we like who we saw? *Isaiah 61:3* reminded us that no matter how the words of our past looked, we had God's promise that He would give us a crown of beauty, to replace the ashes of the past. The three of us clung to those words, knowing we had to make some major changes. We were slowly learning that the Lord was asking for a lifetime commitment of guarding our tongues, not just thirty days.

EVEN IN OUR DISOBEDIENCE, GOD SHOWERS US WITH HIS MERCY

ASSIGNMENT 4

WERE WE LIKE JONAH?

THE FISH

"What sorrow awaits my rebellious children," says the Lord. "You make plans that are contrary to mine. You make alliances not directed by my Spirit, thus piling up your sins." Isaiah 30:1 (NLT)

WERE WE LIKE JONAH?

The word of the Lord came to Jonah son of Amittai: "Go to the great city of Nineveh and preach against it, because its wickedness has come up before me." But Jonah ran away from the Lord and headed for Tarshish. He went down to Joppa, where he found a ship bound for that port. After paying the fare, he went aboard and sailed for Tarshish to flee from the Lord. Jonah 1:1-3 (NIV)

Then they took Jonah and threw him overboard, and the raging sea grew calm. At this the men greatly feared the Lord, and they offered a sacrifice to the Lord and made vows to him. But the Lord provided a great fish to swallow Jonah, and Jonah was inside the fish three days and three nights. Jonah 1:15-17 (NIV)

Then the word of the Lord came to Jonah a second time: "Go to the great city of Nineveh and proclaim to it the message I give you." Jonah obeyed the word of the Lord and went to Nineveh. Now Nineveh was a very important city–a visit required three days. Jonah 3:1-3 (NIV)

The three of us were concerned that our devotion to the Lord was not solid. We knew that God was walking with us every step of the way.

Just as He promised the Israelites that He would be their thunder, fire and cloud to be set before them, He would also be behind us. The Lord continued to speak to us and each time we heard His voice there was conviction that we must respond with childlike faith. The Lord instilled in us to listen, be prepared, stay focused, and not tire or walk where we were not called to fight a battle.

In one of the Bible stories, David had gathered five stones to slay a giant whose name was Goliath. (You can read the entire story in *1 Samuel 17*). Our problem was that we failed to see how that applied to us and our journey. These instructions were foreign to us, and totally out of our comfort zone. God, in His infinite wisdom, sometimes has plans for us that don't always reveal instantaneous answers. The Lord advised us that we would find the answers as we claimed victory over each battle.

September 1 – **"My children, these are My words"**
"Take up your shield, courage and sword. You will have to fight small battles, but you will only need five small stones. I will win. I will determine the end. I will be the thunder, fire, and clouds to be set before you and after you. Now, go in My Name, power, and forget Me not." God

Acknowledging that we had heard from the Lord, each of us prayed for and gathered five small stones that day, as we were instructed to do. In our spirit, the Lord told us that we would be facing five giants on this journey. We didn't know if our giants would be an individual, a business circumstance, health issues, relationships, etc. He assured us that each giant would ultimately be conquered if we listened, prepared ourselves and stayed focused. We would fight several small battles, but it was very evident to us that time was on God's side. The battle and victory ultimately always belongs to the Lord.

> *By day the Lord went ahead of them in a pillar of cloud to guide them on their way and by night in a pillar of fire to give them light, so that they could travel by day or night. Neither the pillar of cloud by day nor the pillar of fire by night left its place in front of the people.*
> *Exodus 13:21-22 (NIV)*

It became very clear to all three of us that the Lord was guiding us into new and uncharted territory. Some may think there are many roads to heaven, with one destination. Remember, the Lord says there is only one road to heaven, which is through Jesus Christ. The path God chose for us to follow would be narrow, which is His road. Patience, trust and obedience to move in His Name and power would be the key to this victory.

The question still remained. What were we going to do with five stones?

September 7–**"My children, these are My words"**

"For today, you are to stay with the cloud and not go forward until I feel you are ready. It will be clear to all of you and you will know then what happens. Read and find out why!

"The next several days will not mean that there is only one day left. One day could mean one week. You need to hear and walk slowly to get the meaning of what I want for you. It is to 'know' that you have accomplished what I need for you to learn for that time. Focus only on My instructions. If you get nothing, then sit and pray longer. Your life, health and progress depend on these next days. Now is your real test of listening. Are you ready to hear? Let My words resonate into your hearts, minds, and souls. Open your eyes and read, study and grasp what you need to learn. I will be the one to tell you when to move, and you will do it without hesitation.

"Now hear My words and instructions, children. You will now walk on a path inside the path. You heard the story of Jonah, but you dismissed it. You will study his short life in detail. All of you will read the book of Jonah, word by word, line by line, and understand fully what happened to him in mind, soul and spirit.

"When I feel you are ready and have received from it what is needed, then and only then will you move on. You will be able to cast My stone and I will remove the cloud that is your first veil to be removed. It is all up to you.

"I don't want you to lead others down the wrong path. Stay on course and listen, pray and be faithful. I know you can, but will you?"

These words from the Lord were gripping and undeniable. We had not listened to His instructions to focus. The Lord was asking us to be "proactive" and more dedicated when telling others about how much He loves them. He wanted unconditional obedience from us. Our mindset was still in the "reactive stage," and we responded with "conditions" attached. We certainly didn't want any negative consequences from the Lord. With the Lord, there are no "conditions." *He will not be manipulated.* After all, He is the Lord God Almighty, the One who calls all the stars by name, and holds the seas in His hand. Who were we to think that we could call the shots on this journey? It was pretty obvious that we were still beginners in learning the art of patience, trust, and obedience. The Lord knew we were not ready to move forward. It was obvious that His words failed to resonate in our hearts, minds and souls, at different times.

The three of us had known and heard about the story of Jonah, but we dismissed it. Why? We were in denial that this story could even resemble our situation. The Lord conveyed to us that we were to study Jonah's short life in detail. We were told to read the book of Jonah, word by word, line by line, and understand fully what happened to him in mind, soul and spirit. For the next four days, we concentrated on each line and verse, trying to identify with Jonah's plight. We, too, were running from God, trying to justify the fact that the responsibilities were too demanding. Little did we know that the Lord's next move for us would ultimately be imbedded in our spirits for the remainder of our days on this earth.

Just as the Lord disciplined Jonah by placing him in the belly of the fish for three days, we too, were about to experience three days living in spiritual bondage because of our disobedience. God told us that we had to be as Jonah, and He placed us spiritually in the belly of the fish. The sensation was as though we had physically been placed in the belly of the fish. For three days, the air around us was sultry, stifling, stale, and heavy. Another analogy of this would be like physically walking into a musty, abandoned building without proper ventilation. During those three days and nights it rained continuously outside of our homes. The sun never appeared from behind the bleak, dismal, gray, ominous looking rain clouds. We remained dysfunctional, confused, discouraged, and overwhelmingly oppressed the entire three days.

During those three days, God reminded us several times, and made it very clear, that *HE WILL BE FIRST IN OUR LIVES.* He had repeatedly communicated that we were to follow Him and do the will of God. We had shown disrespect and disobedience by ignoring those words.

As we sat, secluded from all of the outside influences of our lives, we pleaded for forgiveness and prayed for another chance. However, in all of our confusion, we never repented from our negative actions. Just as the Lord told Jonah, we knew that He had a specific job for us to do. Reluctant to respond, we thought the job looked too hard to complete. Engulfed in a state of spiritual depression, for three days and nights, just like Jonah, we were putting our own interests above the spiritual needs of others around us. God had given us direction through His word and we ran in fear and stubbornness, claiming that God was asking too much from us. Caught up in our own self-righteousness and unfair judgment, we neglected the responsibilities of our journey.

No matter how far all of us try to distance ourselves from Him, *He will find us.*

> *Then if my people who are called by my name will humble themselves and pray and seek my face and turn from their wicked ways, I will hear from heaven and will forgive their sins and restore their land. 2 Chronicles 7:14 (NLT)*

It became apparent that we were becoming too comfortable in thinking that things would be easy. Our agendas and priorities were definitely not in line with God's divine plan. Instead of walking the path of righteousness, we followed our own road. We didn't want to give up our time, nor relinquish our control. Forgiveness certainly wasn't in the picture for us. We weren't willing to acknowledge our rebellion, mistakes, and anger. The Lord saw that self-righteousness was beginning to sneak in around us. As a reminder to us, the Lord had to discipline us for our rebellious ways. Another traumatic lesson learned in the "School of Hard Knocks."

September 12–**"My children, these are My words"**
"My children, do you want to know why you were reading the book of Jonah? I know you do. Now listen carefully.

Were We Like Jonah?

"You were in the book of Jonah because you have been as Jonah. You lived out his life your ways. I wanted you to understand his heart in your times. Now let's go there.

"I gave him a task, he didn't like it, and he ran. I gave the three of you a task and you questioned whether you could do this. I forced Jonah to realize his mistakes and he spent three days in the fish. I forced you three to realize your mistakes and kept you in an unbearable, depressed, mind wandering state for three days. Jonah went to the bottom of the mountains. You went to the pit. When all four of you realized your errors, you began to work through your rebellion. Then, you began to react in rebellious ways, Jonah with the people, and you thinking of rotten, negative things. He became angry and you ate from the rotten fruit on the ground, and all of you became different. When you realized you were wrong, you got up and received My mercy, but still, none of you repented for your actions.

"Jonah's life faded away and you know nothing more about his whereabouts for the rest of his life. Do you want your task to end here, where no one else will know what happens? Are you ready to take another journey to pray for those who are distant from My voice? Yes, I believe you will be ready when the time is right.

"Now, when you look back and think of Jonah, remember the pit, rotten fruit, and disobedience that I do not tolerate. I see all and know all. Don't ever think you can run from Me, or hide from Me. In the book of Jonah I have shown you all My MERCY.

"For now, you will not move another step. The three of you must have patience, pray and listen, and get right with yourselves. The next three days will be a cleansing time for the three of you. Reflect back on all the words, notes, visions and scriptures. I will reveal and put into your hearts what will need to be done in each of your lives. I want your prayers to be direct, merciful and to have purpose. But for today, praise My Holy Name. Sing praises to My Name."

There was a heightened sense that we needed to self-evaluate ourselves. Question after question began to saturate our thoughts. We were very much aware that we had some major decisions to make about our level of trust and our willingness to move forward in obedience with the task that God had given us.

For the next three days we took this time to think about why we were disobedient in our actions. As we looked back on and discussed our past mistakes, we were reminded of the following scripture:

Were We Like Jonah?

> *Measuring as he went, he took me along the stream for 1,750 feet and then led me across. The water was up to my ankles. He measured off another 1,750 and led me across again. This time the water was up to my knees. After another 1,750 feet it was up to my waist. Then he measured another 1,750 feet and the river was too deep to walk across. It was deep enough to swim in, but too deep to walk through.* Ezekiel 47:3-5 (NLT)

Referencing the above scripture, where were we in the river? Up to this point, our actions and reactions had been shallow and insignificant. Were we settling for ankle deep or up to our knees in water? How deep was our commitment to the Lord? As we struggled, were we reluctant to step out in faith? We wondered if we were settling for second best. We had already flinched at seeing that the water was too deep to walk across. We knew there had to be some life-changing decisions. The time had come when we were either going to "sink or swim."

As we wrestled to receive answers, many questions continued to bombard our thoughts. We had been grumbling and complaining up to this point of the journey. How long was the Lord going to tolerate our noncompliance? How much were we learning to control and surrender our mouths? Listening instead of verbalizing each time we were uncomfortable with what was spoken, was not high on our list. What was our tolerance threshold at this point? How does one move in harmony with others when our pride, compassion, humility and words are sometimes not pleasing to the Lord? Is total forgiveness possible to achieve?

So, what did we learn from this experience? It became very clear to us that we needed an "attitude adjustment" to honor and respect the Lord's direction the first time. Sometimes there will be no second chances. We found out that you can't run from God, because there are consequences when you disobey Him. *He will always find you.* Even in your disobedience, God can still use you. No matter where you are, rest assured that God hears your cries. His response will always be in your best interest.

After being humbled and saved by God's grace, once again, we knew we had to make many positive changes to continue with this journey. The many challenges that we would be facing could only be resolved by going to the Lord in fervent prayer. It was our choice how we wanted to pursue the future.

BUT, AS WE KNOW,
GOD ALWAYS HAS THE LAST WORD

ASSIGNMENT 5

"COME TO ME FIRST"

CASTING THE FIRST STONE

No discipline is enjoyable while it is happening – it's painful! But afterward there will be a peaceful harvest of right living for those who are trained in this way. Hebrews 12:11 (NLT)

"COME TO ME FIRST"

May God, who gives this patience and encouragement, help you live in complete harmony with each other, as is fitting for followers of Christ Jesus, Then all of you can join together with one voice, giving praise and glory to God, the Father of our Lord Jesus Christ. Romans 15:5-7 (NLT)

Very early one morning, the Lord revealed to the three of us that we had some work to do to get right with ourselves. Prideful, negative actions were beginning to take a toll on us. Our intolerance of others, as well as with each other, was at a point that the Lord was not pleased with the direction we had taken. We were told to be still, have patience, pray, and listen for instructions from the Lord.

September 12–**"Children, these are My words"**
    "For the next three days this will be your cleansing time. Reflect back on all words, notes, or visions and scriptures. I will reveal and put in

your hearts what will need to be done in each one's life separately. On the fourth day, say a prayer of thanksgiving. On the fifth day, your stone will be cast away and you will need to go forward on My journey, the Path of Holiness, towards My promised land.

"Be still, be ready, and compassionate to yourselves. Listen and learn. Don't be stubborn. Don't dwell if you don't understand. Come to Me, I will answer. Don't fret or get upset. Come to Me! The longer you don't understand or give in, the longer it will take you again. Don't strike the rock I ask you to touch. You have to be made clean. The enemy can't even have a spit of a hold anywhere around you or in you. I need you strong in My Name, not strong in anger. Listen to Me. Open those ears. Blink the eyes that are shut. I do not stand for disobedience, nor can you go any further. These next three days, look into yourselves, for you will need another cleansing of it. Write down what you suffer with now. Let's get it out of the way, totally, no matter who or what. Remember, I know and see all."

The Lord revealed to us that we were to throw our first of five stones in a body of water (a lake) the next morning. When we asked what time of the day we should throw our first stone, His answer was, **"When the dew is on the roses."**–(meaning early morning.)

As we threw the first stone in the water, it created a rippling effect, symbolizing living waters flowing within us. The sun was straight above us and was shining on the water with streams of light in its reflection. He said, **"This is My rock and My fortress, My rod and My staff. I will never leave or forsake you."**

The significance of this act (casting our first stone) was symbolic of our battle/Goliath to release our disobedience and rebellion.

> ...."I will never fail you. I will never abandon you."
> Hebrews 13:5 (NLT)

September 13–**"My children, these are My words"**

"Children. The next thirty days will be testing days. Have you learned? Now you are to put what you have learned to a test. I do not want you to get comfortable in visions, dreams and scriptures. I need you to see and hear more. You must be calm and listen.

"Things have to change. They can't stay as they are now. There is much work to be done, and quickly! Speak the truth with My words.

"Tomorrow as you pray, remember I am the Almighty and I see and hear everything. I know

because I put the thoughts and results into your minds. Remember who you are, 'MY CHILDREN.' I am raising you up to be warriors.

"There will be many distractions. It must be your desire to please Me through your witnessing. When you can help, do it. Don't wait on others. Kind words will be needed. Truth and love must be shown. You won't have to wait for them, as they will be at your back door.

"I want you to be ready. There will be stones thrown. Four other things or obstacles, will be put in your way. It is up to you to notice them. These past three days have been to find your strengths and weaknesses. I will help."

"Don't count your blessings until the four of us have walked the path in which I am leading. You will make it if you concentrate. Things have to be My way or no way at all! Don't lose patience. If you feel uncomfortable, the three of you must talk together.

"I can't afford for any of you to be short-tempered, angry, lonely or hurt. You won't move forward if you are not honest. When My people didn't do what I asked of them, they were put to death either by stoning, fire, sword or the earth parted and engulfed them. Do not let this happen to you! There is too much at stake!"

For the next two days, we read scripture and prayed. During time of prayer, the Lord reminded us that He is the Almighty. He sees everything we do, and hears all that we have released from our mouth. The Lord specifically told us to remember that we are His children. When He told us He was raising us up to be warriors, there was a very uncomfortable feeling that we were not ready for this task. There were too many distractions that had dominated our attention. Many occasions to witness to others had been placed in front of us and we had neglected to act on them. The issue wasn't that we were waiting for the right opportunities, because they were at our back door. The truth was, we often sidestepped our role because it was inconvenient, or we weren't sure of the words to speak. It would have been so easy to speak kind words in love, show a simple smile, or extend a warm hug to a hurting brother or sister. Prideful, self-centered actions kept us from responding in ways that would please the Lord. To be honest with ourselves, we had to openly acknowledge that worldly idols were taking precedence over our obedience to honor the Lord.

September 14–**"My children, these are My words"**

"Each of you must find out for yourself what excess baggage you carry. This is the time it is only about you. You must find out what I need, that only you and I will know.

"Now come to Me, all of you! Pray and talk to Me! First, clear your head, then lay it all out and be true to your heart.

"Take down the wall, come closer, and listen to what I have to say. Be strong and encourage one another. Don't get prideful. Do this with love for each other.

"Find that one special place that gives you peace and comfort, to pray and listen. Don't worry about the surroundings. It is not about that right now, it is about hearing My voice. Now listen and be wise. Do it for Me, not for you!"

Each of us went to our "quiet space" to seek the Lord. It was time that each of us addressed the excess baggage that we carried. The Lord already knew about the flaws that we had so carefully hidden from others. There would be no moving forward on this journey until we acknowledged those negative things that had been bottled up inside of us. This was a time that each of us had to surrender our baggage once and for all. Not only did we have to surrender our own baggage, we had to lend encouragement to each other, as we prayed about and discussed our weaknesses. After confessing our shortcomings, we were amazed that all three of us were carrying similar burdens. These are some of the walls that we built around ourselves:

"Come to Me First"

<u>Judgmental</u>–Often times words of judgment can come back to haunt the one saying them. Sometimes judging others serves only to build up self. There is no such thing as justifiable judgment.

<u>Intolerance</u>–Frequently, when things don't go smoothly, intolerance builds and the situation may intensify. This causes an inability to focus on finding a positive solution.

<u>Not loving our enemies</u> – It is vital to identify the root cause of why there are enemies. In some situations, denial and refusing to acknowledge that there may be a problem keeps a person from reconciliation. Often times it is just a misunderstanding that can be corrected with open and honest dialog and communication.

<u>Depression</u> (low in spirit, agitation) – From time to time, situations arise that can be agitating and cause depression. Sometimes health is a major factor in causing the body to react negatively and the peace of mind is compromised.

<u>Idols</u> (computer, cell phones, TV, sports, cars, food, etc.) – In many instances, many of these can be idols that are very intriguing. These types of idols can dominate time and energy and thus, become negative idols.

<u>Criticism</u> (words and actions) – Occasionally, criticizing serves only to satisfy egos. It is easy to ignore our shortcomings, and there can be a failure to take into consideration how hurtful those words can be to others.

<u>Lack of peace and compassion</u>–At times, a person's life can become so "driven" that there is no time allotted for listening and learning. There is minimal compassion. The main focus often remains on what is best for self, and the desire for peace often escapes the person.

<u>Persecution</u> (harassment) – Sometimes there is an inclination to get very defensive when harassment or persecution takes place. Lifelong scars may result from the failure to recognize that words and

intimidating actions can be very damaging and sometimes non-repairable.

<u>Body and facial language</u>–Learning to control one's body and facial language is not easy to master. Body motions of the head, raising the eyebrows, smiles, frowns, crossing the arms, etc., speak volumes. Without speaking verbally, obvious signals are sent to let others know how a person feels at that particular time.

<u>Being an enabler</u> – An enabler often tries to fix the situation, whether it is asked for or not. By doing this, a lesson that God may be trying to teach someone else could be compromised, or delayed.

<u>Failing to harvest souls</u>.–Thinking that others may not understand or listen creates a heightened tendency to become nervous and apprehensive about witnessing. It often becomes easier to remain silent and passive, rather than speak to others about how much God truly loves each of us.

…I am the Lord, who heals you! Exodus 15:26 (NIV)

The Lord gave one of us words that the enemy had been playing havoc with our minds for years and it was now time to take authority over the situation. The Lord's instructions were to go to a specific location alone and work this out. He stated, **"You have been in the valley for too long, I want you to go to the mountain top. Go to a national cemetery (on a mountain), where you will be with My honored dead. You will not just be with the fallen veterans resting there, but with MY honored dead of times past. You will be with Moses, Aaron, Joshua,**

"Come to Me First"

David, Daniel, and Ruth. Those honored dead will surround you as well."

So, there on that mountain top, along with all of the veterans and His honored dead, a thankful prayer for allowing such an encounter was offered to the Lord.

During the conversation with the Lord, on the mountain that day, the question arose, "What do you expect from us?" His response was very clear, **"Come to Me first in everything. Honor Me, honor your spouse, and honor your spouse's prayers, as they are pleasing to Me."** Continuing, the Lord said, **"Are you willing to follow Me?"** With a quivering voice, the answer was, "Yes." Again, He said, **"NO, ARE YOU WILLING TO FOLLOW ME?"** With more confidence and conviction, the answer was, *"YES, with Your help. It can't be done without You."* Continuing our conversation, the Lord said, **"Before you get angry with what someone says or something that happens, stop and ask if there is a message there from Me."** Kneeling before the Lord on that mountain, heartfelt prayers were lifted up. Crying out for forgiveness was mixed with praises for guiding each of our footsteps during the storms of our lives.

Taking out a small Snickers candy bar to eat, the conversation continued with a question of whether there was a need to thank the Lord for the candy bar. The Lord strongly replied, **"Yes you do! Thank Me for everything, no matter how small or insignificant it seems!"** The Lord's statement brought to mind how often the wonderful blessings we receive are taken for granted, and we fail to thank Him for all that He provides.

"You are on your way, but it will be hard sometimes. Don't get angry with yourself or others. It is time to leave this place now, but try to stay on the mountain top as much as you can."

It was amazing how the Lord had orchestrated that trip to the mountain. That specific day was the High Holy Atonement day of Yom Kippur for the Jewish people. This very day signifies confessing and releasing sins to the Lord. It was an incredible blessing and privilege to have had a conversation with the Lord, on this High Holy Atonement Day.

> *Do not be afraid or discouraged...the battle is not yours, but God's. 2 Chronicles 20:15 (NIV)*

Praise, Honor and Glory belong to You for an enlightening day, Lord Jesus.

COME TO HIM FIRST,
AND BE THANKFUL FOR ALL THINGS

ASSIGNMENT 6

HOW MUCH HE LOVES US

CASTING SECOND STONE THROUGH TREES

I will lead blind Israel down a new path, guiding them along an unfamiliar way. I will brighten the darkness before them and smooth out the road ahead of them. Yes I will indeed do these things; I will not forsake them. Isaiah 42:16 (NLT)

HOW MUCH HE LOVES US

> *This is what the Lord says: "Stop at the crossroads and look around. Ask for the old, godly way, and walk in it. Travel its path, and you will find rest for your souls." Jeremiah 6:16 (NLT)*

The Lord constantly reminded us that He was walking with us, no matter how our day looked. He encouraged us to keep a positive outlook and see the world through His eyes. Our human nature didn't always coincide with that teaching. It was evident that we were still enrolled in the "School of Hard Knocks." However, we were about to encounter God on a new and higher level. In His infinite wisdom and love, God has a way of humbling us, to make us understand that He is the GREAT I AM who loves and cares for us.

September 19–"**My children, these are My words**"
   "**Children: Behind the white clouds are trees, lots of trees. You are on My dirt path, but there are**

twenty rows of green trees. They are to keep you cool and calm as you enter into the next phase.

"Don't look past the trees! Don't try to climb over them! You are to walk through them! I am sheltering you from other things to keep you focused. You will not have to worry about its fruits. Each tree will have a mark on it, which will be a lesson that you must learn. You will receive scriptures and visions.

"With each tree and each lesson, thank Me. As you learn and complete the lesson, the tree will wilt and die. I want you to receive all it has for you, and no one else. When you reach the other side and look back at the path, the trees will have dried, wilted and decayed, signifying that you have learned that lesson and the past is forgotten, never to be remembered again.

"After you have received all My words and scriptures, you will realize who I am. Then and only then, will you move on.

"The second stone will be thrown past the last tree. Then you will once again be ready to continue forward."

After hearing these words from the Lord, the twenty rows of trees seemed to be part of a puzzle that still needed to be put together. The Lord stated to us that we didn't have to worry about the tree's fruit. Not comprehending what all of this meant, the questions began to surface. Would the trees actually have fruit? As we walked through the forest of trees, would the temperature feel hot or sultry? Would there be sounds and smells as the trees fell? The mark on each tree was apparently very significant, because it was the key to another piece of the puzzle. We were told that each mark would be a symbol of a lesson that would be learned. It became obvious to us that there would be twenty lessons to be learned. At that point, we began to understand the significance of the tree wilting and decaying after the lesson was learned. With our limited knowledge, there was a sense that as the trees wilted, the past would be forgotten. We wondered how it was possible that one could completely forget the past, so the peace would come to press into the future.

The Lord's words helped us to understand that to find the answers, it would be necessary to concentrate on the visions and scriptures that we received. As the pieces to the puzzle began to fill in, the anticipation of completing the whole picture piqued our inquisitive minds more than ever. Excitement and adrenalin began to surge, with the expectancy of moving forward on our journey.

You are probably wondering how we knew where to start, when the Lord told us to begin walking through the trees. Please don't stop reading because you don't understand what we are trying to tell you. He tells us it is all right to question. Believing what the Lord told us enabled us to enter the forest of trees, and walk through each lesson.

Taking one lesson a day, we were instructed to study a scripture from the Bible, or meditate on a vision that best described "How much..." On many occasions, all three of us received the same scripture. That was amazing to us. It served as confirmation to know that God orchestrated our inner thoughts, and kept us in tune with each other.

The following are the twenty lessons, visions and scriptures that we received.

HOW MUCH I LOVE YOU:

> *The trumpeters and singers joined in unison, as with one voice, to give praise and thanks to the Lord. Accompanied by trumpets, cymbals and other instruments, they raised their voices in praise to the Lord and sang: "He is good; his love endures forever." 2 Chronicles 5:13 (NIV)*

VISION: Seen in the vision were pliers, wrenches, screwdrivers, and hammers.

INTERPRETATION: Just like these tools are used for a specific purpose, God created us so specifically, that our purpose would not be like any other soul in this universe. He loves us enough to give us our very own DNA, so that each of us is unique in the eyes of the Lord.

Love is such a powerful emotion. It is hard to fathom that God loves us enough to give each of His children individual and unique identities. He keeps all of His children as the apple of His eye (*Psalm 17:8*). How awesome it is to know that His love for us never changes. Down to the last detail, He equips us and supplies our every need.

HOW MUCH I CARE FOR YOU:

> *Give all your worries and cares to God, for he cares about you. 1 Peter 5:7 (NLT)*

VISION: There were legions of angels in the heavens, as far as the eye could see.
INTERPRETATION: Just like the Milky Way has stars too numerous to count, God provides legions of angels as far as the eye can see. The angels are appointed by the Lord, to surround and watch over His children. *God cares enough to send His very best.*

Before God created the universe, He knew all about us. It should not be surprising that He also knew that we would be needing help, guidance and protection as we journeyed through life. To show us how much

He loves and cares for us, He sent His angels to watch over every single detail of our life.

HOW MUCH I WILL TAKE CARE OF YOU:

> *So do not fear, for I am with you; do not be dismayed, for I am your God. I will strengthen you and help you; I will uphold you with my righteous right hand. Isaiah 41:10 (NIV)*

> *Beware that you don't look down on any of these little ones. For I tell you that in heaven their angels are always in the presence of my heavenly Father. If a man has a hundred sheep and one of them wanders away, what will he do? Won't he leave the ninety-nine on the hills and go out to search for the one that is lost? And if he finds it, I tell you the truth, he will rejoice over it more than over the ninety-nine that didn't wander away! In the same way, it is not my heavenly Father's will that even one of these little ones should perish. Matthew 18:10-14 (NLT)*

God cares enough for us to leave the ninety-nine that are saved, and go look for the one that is lost. He will search until He finds that child, and rejoice that the lost is found. God will never run out of love and protection for us, because it comes from a well that never runs dry.

Sometimes the wells of peace, love and faith have a tendency to dry up, because we fail to focus on the One who takes care of our every need. The three of us found ourselves standing before that very well that was beginning to run dry. We had been walking down a path that we had made for ourselves, instead of listening to the voice of the Lord. God sees and hears all of the silent, and sometimes not so silent, cries for help. He is fully capable of getting our attention when we need it. We had been giving God reasons to chase us down while we wandered from His presence. Because He loves and cares for us so intensely, He is willing to wait patiently for us to come back to that well of peace.

HOW MUCH I WILL CLOTHE YOU:

> *Therefore, as God's chosen people, holy and dearly loved, clothe yourselves with compassion, kindness, humility, gentleness and patience. Colossians 3:12 (NIV)*

<u>VISION</u>: We were shown Joseph's coat of many colors.

<u>INTERPRETATION</u>: The colors of the coat were very significant because they represented splendor, righteousness, strength, love, compassion, humility, and dignity. *Red*: Blood remembrance – Jesus; *Purple*: Priestly; *Green*: Green pastures/rest; *Blue*: Living waters, Holy Spirit; *Yellow*: God's radiance; *Orange*: Righteousness.

In the Bible story of Joseph in *Genesis 37*, it tells how his father provided him a coat of many colors. What a beautiful coat that must have been. Imagine our Heavenly Father giving us a beautiful coat with colors so magnificent that there were no words to describe them. Perhaps the radiant colors of one of

God's rainbows might be one of many illustrations of that beauty. God clothes us with His majestic splendor each and every day

HOW MUCH I SEE YOU:

> ...*The Lord doesn't see things the way you see them. People judge by outward appearance, but the Lord looks at the heart. 1 Samuel 16:7 (NLT)*

The Lord instructed the three of us to write in our journal each day. As we reviewed our daily notes, we found the following entry:

He sees our heart.
He sees our hurts.
He sees our weaknesses.
He sees our strengths.
He sees our joy.
He sees our pain.
He sees our compassion.
He sees our faults.
He sees our enthusiasm.
He sees our worship.
He sees our anger.
He sees our frustrations.
He sees our love for our families.
He sees our love for others.
He sees our peace.
He sees us ask for forgiveness and repentance.

He sees our face.
AND – HE STILL LOVES US.

We should remember that God always sees everything and hears all. No matter how we act, we can't hide any of our thoughts or actions from Him. God always sees our goodness as well as our faults. In spite of the times that we tend to drift from His presence, He continually showers His blessings and unconditional love on us.

HOW MUCH I WATCH OVER YOU:

Psalm 121:3 through 8, reminds us of the Lord's faithfulness to watch over us:

> *He will not let your foot slip – he who watches over you will not slumber... The Lord watches over you – the Lord is your shade at your right hand; the sun will not harm you by day, nor the moon by night. The Lord will keep you from all harm – he will watch over your life; the Lord will watch over your coming and going both now and forever. Psalm 121:3... 8 (NIV)*

Lord, as You protect our hearts, You also heal old scars that make their way to the surface and erupt. You hide us under the shadow of Your wings. No matter how many times we stray from Your voice, You watch over us and pull us back so we can hear You again. We realize and acknowledge how kind, tolerant and patient You are with us Lord. Thank you for Your mercy and grace.

HOW MUCH I WILL FEED YOU:

> ***"Therefore, I tell you, do not worry about your life, what you will eat or drink, or about your body, what you will wear. Is not life more important than food, and the body more important than clothes?"*** *Matthew 6:25-27 (NIV)*

Occasionally, while trying to arrange the details of our lives, God is left out of the equation. There are times that we try to make things happen on our own. Jesus made it very clear that He would provide for our every need. Sometimes we worry so much about our everyday life, we neglect to rely upon and thank Him for all of the things He provides. The abundant blessings that God showers upon us, constantly feeds and clothes our minds, bodies, souls, and spirits, even if we sometimes fail to recognize those promises.

HOW HE SUPPLIES US:

> *And my God will meet all your needs according to his glorious riches in Christ Jesus.*
> *Philippians 4:19 (NIV)*

God's promise is whatever we need on earth He will always supply, even if we need courage in the face of danger or discomfort. He also tells us that He will supply everything we need in heaven. We must remember, however, that there is a difference between our wants and our needs. We may not get all we want, but He will always give us exactly what we need, in His time. The three of us thanked God that He doesn't give us all that for which we prayed. Sometimes good intentions can turn into selfish and self-centered prayers. God chose the path for each of us before we were even born. He knows our every need before we even ask, and never makes mistakes when answering our prayers.

HOW HE GIVES US FOOD:

> *After all, our ancestors ate manna while they journeyed through the wilderness! The Scriptures say, 'Moses gave them bread from heaven to eat."* **Jesus said, "I tell you the truth, Moses didn't give you bread from heaven. My Father did. And now He offers you the true bread from heaven. The true bread of God is the one who comes down from heaven and gives life to the world."** *John 6:31-33 (NLT)*

God also provides us with spiritual food of wisdom, knowledge and discernment. The Lord revealed one vision that helped us comprehend how He gives life to the world.

VISION: We sensed that we were being taken to the "Valley of the Dry Bones." In that valley was a small piece of desert that was dry, lifeless, and had one pile of bones. (We could sense several piles of bones around us, but could not see them.) From the one pile of bones that we saw, the bones began to move slightly, into the shape of a human skeleton. The bones were not connected, nor did they have flesh. (We were allowed to see the bones only from the waist down.)

<u>INTERPRETATION:</u> God is beginning to bring life back into His people. The reason we could not see the upper half of the skeleton was because the mind, heart, spirit and soul of the people had not been fed the Word of God. They were lacking the spiritual food needed to "stand up and fight for the Lord." However, there was evidence that God had begun the process of healing. *Praise God Almighty.*

At times the three of us had been that pile of dry bones, alive in the body, but dry in the spirit. Our Father in heaven offers all of us the true bread from heaven. God is faithful to provide food for the body and spiritual nurturing for the soul. This was a blatant reminder that on this journey, our spiritual bones had sometimes lacked the nourishment to 'stand up and fight for the Lord.'

HOW WE WILL NOT BE THIRSTY:

> *On the last day, that great day of the feast, Jesus stood and cried out, saying,* **"If anyone thirsts, let him come to Me and drink. He who believes in Me, as the Scripture has said, out of his heart will flow rivers of living water."**
> *John 7:37-38 (NKJV)*

The words, 'come and drink' alludes to the Messiah's life-giving blessings in promising to give the Holy Spirit to all who believe. Jesus uses the term 'living water' to indicate life eternal. The two go together. God will never send a thirsty soul to a dry well. It is a wonderful concept to realize that if we search for the 'living water,' we have the opportunity to spend eternity with our Lord and Savior.

HOW WE WILL NOT HUNGER:

> *He upholds the cause of the oppressed and gives food to the hungry..... Psalm 146:7 (NIV)*

God doesn't separate the physical food from the spiritual food. The thing is, God doesn't yell out at us and say *"Hey, you are neglecting Me. Sit down and listen for a while so you can hear Me."* He wants us to willingly give Him some time during the day to quietly speak to us. God desires that we hunger for the sound of His voice. The food that only God can provide brings wholeness to the body, mind and spirit. Will God speak to you if you let Him? Most definitely. Not only in an audible voice, but through your thoughts and emotions. At times, the three of us were negligent in making God our first priority. Because of that, sometimes our minds and emotions were void of that inner peace and quiet and assurance that only God can give.

HOW HE WILL PREPARE A PLACE FOR US:

> *"See, I am sending an angel before you to protect you on your journey and lead you safely to the place I have prepared for you....."*
> *Exodus 23:20 (NLT)*

> **"Do not let your hearts be troubled. Trust in God; trust also in me. In my Father's house are many rooms; if it were not so, I would have told you. I am going there to prepare a place for you. And if I go and prepare a place for you, I will come back and take you to be with me that you also may be where I am. You know the way to the place where I am going."** *John 14:1-4 (NIV)*

God has already prepared a special place in our heart that we can retreat (go to) and commune (worship/praise) with Him. It is a safe place where each of us can be ALONE with God. We don't have to be concerned that others will hear our cries and our praises. We can't find that room for you, and you will not know where that room is that others share with God. He prepares that place for each individual. Once each of us finds that intimate, secret place in our heart/soul, we can expect to experience a peace that surpasses all human understanding. Sometimes, the light grows dim, and may completely fade away in our secret space, and we get lost and wander for a time. But, when we do find our way back, we know for certain that God always leaves the light on for us. God patiently waits there to unconditionally love on each of us. The times that we need God the most is when we think we don't need Him. He is our friend who never leaves us. We can go to Him many times each day, knowing that He will always be there to welcome us. We are called to be a light in the darkness, without apology or fear. Thank You, Lord, for preparing a place for each of us to meet with You.

HOW HE DEMANDS OUR LOVE:

> *Do not worship any other god, for the Lord, whose name is Jealous, is a jealous God.*
> *Exodus 34:14 (NIV)*

Pagan worship cannot be mixed with the worship of the Holy God. Jesus very blatantly pointed out, **"No one can serve two masters...."** (*Matthew 16:24*). We cannot serve both God and pagan idols. He demands that we have no other gods before Him. We think of idols as statues of wood or stone, but in reality an idol is anything natural that is given sacred value and power. God commands us to live and serve only under the authority of the Lord, Jesus Christ, God Almighty.

HOW HE DEMANDS OUR FAITHFULNESS:

> *He has showed you, O man, what is good. And what does the Lord require of you? To act justly and to love mercy and to walk humbly with your God. Micah 6:8 (NIV)*

THOUGHTS TO PONDER:
God demands our faithfulness in:
Tithing in prayer life
Service to others
Helping the poor
Loving our family
Obedience in listening
Being faithful in forgiveness
Putting God first in everything
Humbling ourselves before God
Keeping commandments and laws
Receiving God's discipline and correction
Discover what pleases God, then make them habits
Making time to sit with the Lord to just hang out with Him

HOW HE IS FAITHFUL:

> *Know therefore, that the Lord your God is God; he is the faithful God, keeping his covenant of love to a thousand generations of those who love him and keep his commands. Deuteronomy 7:9 (NIV)*

VISION: There was a woman sitting on a rock at the top of a mountain, with her arms leaning on her knees. She was gazing, in amazement, at the mountains and valleys that the Lord had created. "**Look around!**" the Lord said. In another area, crowds of people were looking toward the mountains, praising God for the beauty of His creation.

INTERPRETATION: We should stand in awe of the Creator of our universe. It is God's desire to let us know that He provides such beauty and splendor, because He loves His children so much. He is faithful in the little things, as well as the big things. Even the air we breathe is a faith gift from God.

Imagine yourself driving through the mountains on a crisp autumn day. You have planned the trip to coincide with the changing of the leaves. As you drive on the winding roads, the beauty and splendor of the entire mountainside scenery is overwhelmingly breathtaking. The leaves look as though the Creator of our universe took His paintbrush and painted the leaves with brilliant colors of yellow, gold, red, orange, rust and brown. It is hard to comprehend that God loves each of us so much that He created and showers us with such magnificent beauty. Each new day is full of His promises and faithfulness to love on His children. He is still a God of miracles.

HOW HE IS ALMIGHTY:

> ...."Holy, holy, holy is the Lord God, the Almighty – the one who always was, who is, and who is still to come." Revelation 4-8 (NLT)

Genesis 1-31 tells us about the mighty power and glory of the Lord God Almighty, and how in six days, He created the universe.

Day 1 – Light, Darkness
Day 2 – Sky and Water (waters separated)

Day 3 – Land, Seas, (waters gathered) Vegetation
Day 4 – Sun, Moon, Stars (govern day and night, seasons, days and years)
Day 5 – Fish, Birds (to fill waters and sky)
Day 6 – Animals, (fill the earth) Man and Woman (care for earth, commune with God)
Day 7 – God rested and declared everything He made to be very good.

God didn't just create the world, He carefully and intricately designed it.

HOW HE WILL NEVER LET US GO

> .....*"Never will I leave you; never will I forsake you."* Hebrews 13:5(NIV)

VISION: We were in deep water, over our heads. We had on life jackets, with the name "Jesus" written on them. Jesus was holding on to us by our shirt collars. He was walking on water and dragging us through the water. He said, **"You will get to the other side as long as you focus on Me."** INTERPRETATION: No matter how deep you are in turbulent circumstances, focus on Jesus and He will rescue you.

At times the three of us were insensitive to circumstances that were placed before us. It was easier to drift into our own little self-centered world than to address our negligence. On occasion, we lost our focus to rely on the One who holds our hands and our hearts in the palm of His hand. God is always ready to rescue us, even when we are weak and fail to trust His promises. The Lord tells us that He will never leave us. *We should believe and receive.*

HOW HE GIVES US OUR DESIRES:

> *Delight yourself in the Lord and he will give you the desires of your heart. Psalm 37:4 (NIV)*

Everything we have or do should be committed to the Lord. Devoting ourselves to Him means entrusting everything – our lives, families, jobs, finances, and possessions, to His control and guidance. This happens only when we know Him better.

HOW HE HEALS US:

> *Don't be impressed with your own wisdom. Instead, fear the Lord and turn away from evil. Then you will have healing for your body and strength for your bones. Proverbs 3:7-8 (NLT)*

<u>VISION 1</u>: Seen was an onion that was ready to be peeled, layer by layer.

<u>INTERPRETATION</u>: The Lord said the healing would take place in layers. He disclosed that it would be like peeling an onion. Peeling after peeling (ten or twelve layers) from the onion slowly drifted like white clouds, toward the heavens. Each peeling represented healing in one form or another.

<u>VISION 2</u>: Before us was a turtle. The turtle was lying upside down on the hard shell. It was kicking its legs, trying to turn itself upright. We sensed that it would be a slow process, but eventually something would come along to help the turtle get itself upright. Only then, would it be able to move forward.

<u>INTERPRETATION</u>: This is patience. We are all broken vessels that God wants to use for His glory. Healing is a process that takes patience, which is coordinated and completed in God's perfect timing.

Healing comes in many different forms. Some may need physical healing, while others might need emotional or spiritual release and healing. All require patience and prayer, and a willingness to trust God's perfect timing for our answers. Do we find that easy to do? Not always. Sometimes it is just like peeling layer after layer from the onion, it is a process! True prayer does not evade pain, but gains from it insight, patience, courage and sympathy. When we pray, we release the power of heaven into our lives.

HOW HE IS WHO HE SAYS HE IS:

> .... *"I AM WHO I AM"*.... *God also said to Moses, "Say to the Israelites, 'The Lord, the God of your fathers – the God of Abraham, the God of Isaac and the God of Jacob – has sent me to you.' This is my name forever, the name by which I am to be remembered from generation to generation."*
> *Exodus 3-14-15 (NIV)*

God is a jealous God, and the name **"I AM WHO I AM"** will forever be remembered from generation to generation. We were definitely struggling in the "School of Hard Knocks."

September 28–**"My children, these are My words"**
   "What happens next? Don't ask! Do you want to complete this task or not?

   "Is it foolish to you because you don't understand?

   "If I give you the results, will you still do My work, and go on?

   "If you continually ask why or how, when I have given you the answers, then you haven't learned anything!

   "Why are you questioning Me?

   "Don't you see miracles already?

   "Are you committed, no matter what?

   "Do you still want to go on even if you don't know how, why, or can you?

   "Well, what are your answers?

   "Learn who I am – you will need it after the task of twenty days.

   "Things will be harder. You must get stronger, wiser and go deeper.

   "Get ready! Deliverance is on its way from all sides. There will be many darts thrown at you. What you learn now is how they will pass you by.

You need to be strong and mighty to dodge the darts. Don't be on the wrong side of the stones, like Goliath. You may be strong and mighty together, but you can also come down together. Do not leave My sight! Don't try to hide from Me! I need you as much as you need Me.

"One day at a time! One day at a time!"

Once again, it was as though our minds began to shut down when we didn't like what we were hearing. Even when we heard the Lord's stern words, we continued to ask Him many questions that we had repeated over and over for several months. Just as the Israelites wandered through the desert for forty years, we complained that we were still wandering through this same modern day desert. For what reason were we doing this? What was going to happen? How long would we be on this journey? The Lord had spoken to us many times before, and we were still looking for more confirmation about the journey. When were we going to learn that being disobedient always produces consequences?

It was very obvious that the journey was getting harder to walk in obedience. All three of us agreed that we must surrender all of the negative thoughts and doubts. We had to concentrate on how to get stronger, wiser, and go deeper in our relationship with the Lord.

The Lord once again reminded us of His earlier words to us. We were not to look past the trees, or try to climb over them! His instructions were to walk through them. (The Lord was referring to the twenty lessons that we had to learn before we could move on. Each of those trees ultimately held the secret to our success.) The grace of God sheltered us from other things to keep us focused on this assignment.

September 30–**"My children, these are My words"**
"After you throw your second stone through the trees, you will face your Goliath. The three of you need to bring it down. It will try to throw darts and spears at you from all angles. You are now learning how to fight it. It is much taller and bigger than you, but you have My words and promises. You will need to slay it!

"Continue to pray with magnitude. Don't ever forget that I need you to be strong at this time. Learn and remember! Continue on this path!

"The further ahead you all move, the more things will be revealed. You will begin to see and understand what it is you are doing. This is not only for you, the church and my children, but for Me. It is a testimony of My works and promises.

You will be glad you finished. Now, be silent and continue to pray. Your Goliath will be revealed."

Indeed, many darts had been thrown at the three of us. The lesson to be learned now was how to be strong and mighty to dodge the darts so they would not harm us. There was a concern that if we didn't listen and learn this time, we would be on the wrong side of the stones, like Goliath. Just as the Lord commanded, the lessons would have to be learned *"One day at a time."* The next three days were spent lifting our concerns up to the Lord in prayer.

According to the Lord's instructions, each of us pitched our second stone into a grove of trees. The Lord, our Protector, went before us through the forest of trees. As each tree fell and the path was ultimately cleared, we learned how to fight and conquer the fiery darts that were constantly thrown at us. Through God's words and promises, we received strength, wisdom, and peace to obtain victory. This battle/Goliath symbolized the release of all fears and doubts that had been bottled up inside of us.

October 3–**"My children, these are My words"**
   "Children: Now you know what I mean when I say 'Keep Clean.' You do hear My voice. You do know My words. You do know to fear Me. You are

on the path of holiness. You have come to Me quicker than before.

"I love each and all of My children. I am a God of love. I am a God of restoration. I hear your cries and know your pain. It is well with you, because you are learning.

"Pain is received, so you can heal...and you will! I have you covered, and I will heal you from this situation. Time after time, you will see Me and My works.

"Now, let us move forward!"

For the next several days, we prayed prayers of protection and safety for ourselves. There was a strong sense that another pivotal change in our lives was about to happen.

We don't ever have to fear the sound of hoof beats (**"FAITHFUL AND TRUE" – "RIDING ON A WHITE HORSE"–"THE WORD OF GOD,"** three of many names for God) if we keep our eyes fastened to the One who holds the reins.

GOD IS THE GREAT "I AM"- WE ARE NOT

ASSIGNMENT 7

WHY DID WE WORRY?

STICK MAN

"Therefore I tell you, do not worry about your life, what you will eat or drink; or about your body, what you will wear. Is not life more important than food and the body more than clothes?..." Matthew 6:25-27 (NIV)

WHY DID WE WORRY?

"Therefore, do not worry about tomorrow, for tomorrow will worry about itself. Each day has enough trouble of its own."
Matthew 6:34 (NIV)

The Lord directed us to take an unusual, but very interesting, change of direction for several days. Knowing that we were headed in a different direction, we struggled (worried) with thoughts that our faith might not be strong enough to follow Him. God wanted to release that worry from us, and allowed us to receive this next assignment.

Worry is one of the leading causes of anxiety. We worry when our bodies do not function normally. Allowing our mind to go in all directions may cause a negative reaction, and the physical symptoms can get blown out of proportion. At times, we let our mind leap from problem to problem, tangling our thoughts in anxious knots. Our thoughts consume us, and eventually those negative thoughts cause false symptoms in certain parts of our body. The only remedy is to switch our focus from the problem to the presence of God.

God is all about positive change, and our only responsibility was to follow His lead. We learned in new ways that our bodies are sacred temples, to be used to glorify the Lord. The body is a unit, though it is made up of many parts.

Our instructions were to research and select scriptures throughout the Bible that referenced each of the parts of the body listed below. He wanted us to identify and learn how each part functioned in relationship with the rest of the body. The purpose of this assignment was quite evident. Knowing the functions of each part of the body, we could encourage others with scriptural knowledge, regarding their infirmities, when we prayed with them.

For three days, we prayed for our specific worries. We were definitely concerned about our "What If's." The Lord showed us that He is a God of "If Whats." **"If what I say is not done..."** From that day forward, these words became embedded in our minds throughout our journey. We still look back on that day and remember that statement.

October 7–**"My children, these are My words"**

"WORRY!!! It is big! You continually worry about your families. What is the outcome of this journey? The church? Who will be with us at the end? Will each of you get healed? Worry is a continuous battle.

"For the next few days, we will work on 'worry,' and how you must release it. I need you to give it up, and not let it be the part of your lives that dominates you. Write down ALL of your worries. I mean every single one of them – large or small."

You must be wondering where we are going with this scenario. We knew that obedience was the key factor in moving ahead. We will now attempt to explain how we moved forward with this particular assignment.

We were given a strange symbol that resembled a "stick man." This made no sense to us until we drew the symbol on a piece of paper and studied it for some time.

October 8–**"My children, these are My words"**
"The figure of worry:
"'W' – is the top part of the body with the arms lifted to the Lord.
"'O'–is the head on top of the "W.

"'R'–the lowercase 'r' that is backward and facing the opposite side, is the upper part of the body.

"'R'–the second lowercase 'r' that is written the correct way, is the bottom part of the body.

"'Y'–the 'Y' is upside down, and are the legs of the body. The long line of the 'Y' is the line that reaches up to the head, and holds the body together."

October 11 – **"Pray for safety for yourselves all day, as there is a ten-foot Goliath standing in front of you."**

October 12 – **"Write out your worries, every single one, large or small."**

October 13 – **"Pray for you to receive scriptures, visions and words."**

October 14–**"Come together to pray for each of these worries."**

October 15–**"Start to pray for the letters: Today pray for the 'O.' These are the worries in your mind and facial expressions/emotions."**

October 16 – **"Pray for the letter 'W.' These are worries in the heart and upper part of your bodies."**

October 17 – **"Pray for the first lowercase 'r.' These are the worries of the upper stomach and all of the upper parts of the body."**

October 18–"**Pray for the second lowercase 'r.' These are worries of the lower (colon area) stomach and the surrounding parts of the body.**"

October 19 – "**Pray for the upside down part of the 'Y.' These are worries of all the parts of the legs.**"

October 20–"**Pray for the stem of the 'Y.' These are worries that go up the body (spine) that holds it together.**"

October 21 – "**Praise Me all day.**"

October 22–"**CAST YOUR THIRD STONE! (Instructions) Wrap the words of worry that you wrote down around the third stone, and cast the stone into a dumpster. Do not throw the stone into your own trash dumpster. The words around the stone will deteriorate in a landfill, and will no longer be remembered.**

"Children, I know that worry is a gene that you all have and the flesh keeps it there. It can hinder your lives. I need you to be able to get through it and release it before it cripples you. Your minds can't go there. There will be concerns, but don't let it paralyze you.

"Walk with Me! Learn to walk in My light! You are getting there. It will take some time, but in the end, you will be resurrected.

"Thank you for your obedience and faithfulness. Both are growing you and you will feel how it overtakes your lives, to be the people I can rely upon.

"Go in peace and in My love." Lord, Christ Jesus.

Remember how you were encouraged by a leader who realized your potential to move ahead? This person was someone who believed you could do the task that was given to you, and would support you all of the way? In *Jeremiah 29:11*, we are told that God is that leader. He knows the plans that He has for us. They are plans for good and not for disaster. Those plans are to give all of us a future and a hope. After reading that scripture, the three of us knew that as long as we followed God's agenda, we would complete this mission. Because it was so out of the ordinary, we wondered how we would be able to comprehend the purpose and be able to move forward. The Lord said that He would not show us what was on the road ahead, but His promise was that He would thoroughly equip us for the journey.

During our quiet time, we prayed for understanding and wisdom to accomplish those things that God was asking us to do. There was an awareness that we would need strict discipline to complete this assignment.

The three of us acknowledge that there are many scriptures relating to the body that may have special meaning for you, and they would be quite different from those we have chosen. Several scriptures that we chose had a lasting impact on the three of us. We were absolutely amazed at the number of times body parts and their functions were mentioned in both the Old and New Testaments.

We were given six days to complete this portion of the assignment. The Lord's instructions were to research every single word listed from the word WORRY, and find a scripture that confirmed a connection to that word in the Bible. Sometimes the Lord revealed the scripture in our spirit, and other times we had to find the scripture on our own. Several of the passages we chose had the exact word attached to the scripture. Others only had a connection to the general location of the part of the body.

As we journey through the body, you will notice that we are beginning with the letter "O," which represents the head. We suggest that you refer to the illustration of the "stick man" that is shown in the beginning of this particular assignment. As we move through the body, the letters will take on the shape of a "stick man."

Please join us on our trip through the body.

<u>"O"–HEAD</u>
- Hair . . . . .Matthew 10:30
- Boils . . . . .Leviticus 13:18-19
- Temple. . . . . .Revelation 9:4

Mind	Timothy 1:7
Thoughts	Isaiah 55:8
Ears	Matthew 11:15
Eyes	Luke 11:34-36
Nose	Genesis 2:7
Eye Brows	Leviticus 14:8-9
Cheeks	Luke 6:29
Jaws	Psalm 3:7
Teeth	Psalm 3:7
Tongue	Proverbs 12:18
Mouth	Proverbs 21:23
Lips	Psalm 63:3
Throat	Psalm 63:3

During the time of investigating the different parts of the body in the Bible, from the throat upward, there was a conscious effort to observe facial expressions. The "O" representing the head shows others the individual's character, personality and mannerisms. By watching one's expressions, moods of frustration, pain, sadness, joy, anger, tears, excitement, peace, etc., all can be distinguished in that person. The face, just like a book, gives many details and insights if it is read. The head holds the key to the success of the rest of the body. God, in His infinite wisdom, gave us a sound mind, our thoughts, eyes to see, ears to hear, mouth/lips/throat to speak and taste. All of the above listed features are, in part, what enables us to have spiritual, physical and emotional health. It was overwhelming to think that our Heavenly Father carefully and lovingly designed all of these characteristics before we were even born.

"W"–HEART AND UPPER BODY

Neck	Proverbs 6:20-21
Shoulders	Luke 15:4-5
Arms	Numbers 11:23
Elbows	Psalm 44:3
Hands	Jeremiah 18:6
Fingers	Deuteronomy 9:10
Nails	Daniel 4:33
Chest	Revelation 1:12-13
Heart	Acts 1:24
Muscles	Ezekiel 37:6
Thyroid	Psalm 115:3-7
Upper Lungs	Job 27:3-4
Ribs	Genesis 2:21-22
Esophagus	1 Timothy 5:23

Continuing with the scripture research of the body parts, there was an overwhelming sense of awe at the reality of how much God loves and blesses His children every single day. We all need to love and be loved by others. One of the beautiful gifts that God gave us was a heart that is capable of extending compassion, discernment, joy, peace, and most of all, love. Sometimes we forget how to love with a purpose. When that happens, we may be called to reevaluate our actions and deeds to see where we can make better decisions. The Lord may allow our hearts to be totally broken for a time, or even for a season. When that happens, He could be telling us to sweep all of the corners and wash the windows (wipe away the pain) of that broken heart. God wants all of us to see others as He sees and loves us. The beautiful part of this is, God loves us enough to mend our heart and sew it back up with thread laced with joy, enthusiasm, hope, peace, confidence and love. *Imagine that concept of healing.*

There are times when each of us goes through trials and our hearts are heavy for one reason or another. During those times, we long for a hug, or shoulder to lean on. God knew all of this and created strong arms to hug, and gentle, loving hands to help those who need love. Without the other parts of the upper body to assist in helping the arms and hands to move with precision, many hugs would go undelivered.

If we strive to have healthy bodies and keep our minds clear, it may be easier to recognize the opportunities to assist in taking the burden off the shoulders of those less fortunate. In your mind, think

Why Did We Worry?

about how you might use your hands, arms, shoulders, muscles, etc., to glorify God. It blesses Him so much, to see how creative we can be in the ways we serve Him.

BACKWARD "R"–UPPER STOMACH
    Liver . . . . Exodus 29:13
    Stomach . . . . Mark 7:18-19
    Diaphragm. . . . . Genesis 2:7
    Ribs . . . . Genesis 2:21-22
    Gall bladder. . . . . Leviticus 8:18-21
    Kidneys . . . . Exodus 29:13
    Pancreas . . . . Leviticus 4:8-10
    Hiatal Hernia . . . . Revelation 21:4
    Colon . . . . Leviticus 9:12-14

If you live in a building owned by someone else, you try not to violate the building's rules. What an awesome thought to know that God is our Resident Landlord. He is ever faithful, by making provision throughout the entire body.

The upper stomach parts are vital to one's overall health. Sometimes the pain that overrides our well being is intimidating and keeps us focused on self. Many of these parts filter the abnormal infections that plague the body and sometimes cause fearful reactions. By striving to keep a positive attitude and maintaining healthy eating habits, there is freedom to look beyond the walls of one's body to reach out to others. Others may need encouragement to help them with their own health issues. It is very easy to forget that we don't even move, or breathe, without the blessing of the Lord. Because our body belongs to God, we must not violate His standards for living.

The scripture in *1 Corinthians 6:19* reminds us that the body is the temple of the Holy Spirit, who lives in us and is given to us by God (our Resident Landlord.) We do not belong to ourselves, because God bought us with a high price. We must honor Him with our body.

FRONTWARD "R"–LOWER STOMACH

Lower Back Muscles. . .Isaiah 8:17
Rectum . . . . .2 Chronicles 21:12-18
Spleen . . . . .Leviticus 3:13
Ovaries . . . . .Genesis 3:16
Small Intestine. . . . . . .Leviticus 1:13
Urethra . . . . .Leviticus 3:9
Thighs . . . . .Revelation 19:16
Appendix . . . . .Revelation 21:4
Sciatica Nerve . . . . . . .Revelation 21:4
Bladder . . . . .Leviticus 3:9
Coccyx. . . . . .Leviticus 8:18-21

Why Did We Worry?

The scripture located in *1 Corinthians 12:23-24* states that we are to respect and honor all parts of our body. The Frontward "R" (Lower Stomach) specifically addresses those presentable and unpresentable parts. Many of the words of the lower stomach are very private/personal and unspoken in mixed company conversations. Because the parts are unpresentable, weak and indispensable, they are to be treated with special modesty, while our presentable parts need no special treatment. Without the support of these vital lower stomach parts, the remainder of the body would be unable to function.

"Y"–KNEE/LEG

All Leg Bones in Knees . Daniel 6:10
Knees. . . . . .Romans 14:11
Tibia . . . . .Ezekiel 37:4
Fibula . . . . .Ezekiel 37:4
Femur . . . . .Ezekiel 37:4
Tendons. . . . . .Ezekiel 37:4
Biceps . . . . .Ezekiel 37:4
Shin Bone . . . . .Ezekiel 37:4
Calf . . . . .Leviticus 1:9
Ankle. . . . . .Ezekiel 47:3-6
Feet . . . . .Psalm 119:105
Toes. . . . . .Leviticus 8:22-24
Nails . . . . .Leviticus 8:22-24

The knees, legs, thighs, and feet are the weight bearers and are designed to be the support system for the entire body. It blesses God when those of us with healthy bodies help those who have ailments, such as feeble knees and weak hands. These specific parts encourage the body to draw strength to carry the load for those who are broken, helpless, hopeless, and lack the endurance to carry the load themselves.

The Bible story of Jonah was a blatant reminder that he ran from the Lord out of disobedience. Jonah was able-bodied, but refused to acknowledge the call that was placed on his life. There is such a great lesson to be learned from Jonah's life. As long as our legs and feet will carry us, we should never run from, nor turn our backs on anyone who needs encouragement and support. We can all be the hands and feet of Christ. (Meaning do as Jesus did, as He walked this earth.)

<u>SPINE</u>
    Spine Disc . . . . Luke 13:10-13
    Cartilage . . . . Luke 13:10-13
    Backbone. . . . . Leviticus 3:9

It is amazing to think about how God made the human body. Just as the well-oiled parts of a machine move with accuracy, God created our bodies to move with precision so that each part of the body is in alignment to work together. The spine is the backbone of the entire body, and it controls all parts. Each vertebrae is a gift to a specific area of the body. When one vertebrae is weak, it inhibits the rest of the body from doing its job. Health is one of our greatest God-given assets. The healthier one stays, the easier it is to remain stable during life's storms.

This prompted the saying, "Don't let us be spineless." (Meaning don't let us be so weak that we won't stand up and fight for ourselves or for others.) We can be the spiritual 'backbone' for others by staying in the Word, praying for, and encouraging those who need a warm hug, a shoulder to lean on, or friendly smile.

BODY

> *Now the body is not made up of one part but of many. If the foot should say, "Because I am not a hand, I do not belong to the body," it would not for that reason cease to be part of the body. And if the ear should say, "Because I am not an eye, I do not belong to the body," it would not for that reason cease to be part of the body. If the whole body were an eye, where would the sense of hearing be? If the whole body were an ear, where would the sense of smell be? But in fact God has arranged the parts in the body, every one of them, just as he wanted them to be. If they were all one part, where would the body be? As it is, there are many parts but one body. The eye cannot say to the hand, "I don't need you!" And the head cannot say to the feet, "I don't need you!"*

> *On the contrary, those parts of the body that seem to be weaker are indispensable, and the parts that we think are less honorable we treat with special honor. And the parts that are unpresentable are treated with special modesty, while our presentable parts need no special treatment. But God has combined the members of the body and has given greater honor to the parts that lacked it, so that there should be no division in the body, but that its parts should have equal concern for each other. If one part suffers, every part suffers with it; if one part is honored, every part rejoices with it. 1 Corinthians 12:14-26 (NIV)*

This scripture is showing us that each of us is a member of the Body of Christ. We are all baptized by one Holy Spirit, into one body. The body is a unit, although made up of many parts, they form one body, but we don't lose our individual identity. We may have different interests and gifts, but we all share the same Spirit, which means that each of us has received the same Holy Spirit.

What would the response be if one member was honored? How would we respond if someone was suffering? Are we happy to be with those who are happy? If they were sad, would we share their sorrow? Is there a sense of apathy toward those who weep? We are all in this world together. There is no such thing as a private or individualistic member of the Body of Christ. God is calling us all to get involved in the lives of others and not just enjoy our own relationship with the Lord.

These scriptures brought more questions to the surface, as we searched for answers. Were our eyes (spiritual understanding) sending a beacon of light to others? Were we hiding our knowledge (witnessing) from others? Did others see light in us? Did our character reflect humbleness when we spoke? Did our pride and character continue to leap out at people? Were we obedient to stand in the gap for our brothers and sisters in Christ? Did our shadows cast darkness or light? Would people really want to gravitate to us? Were we genuinely compassionate enough?

These heart-stirring questions were very thought-provoking. As we prayed for answers, the Lord prompted us to examine our own hearts and motives, to put these questions to rest.

We have been, and are, on this journey about the "body," and the purpose of this assignment is to be able to help the Body of Christ (His people) through difficult times.

Each time we received messages from the Lord, we were overwhelmed at the words He spoke. Sometimes the words were of praise, and other times they were of discipline or reprimand because of our disobedience to follow instructions. We were continuously asking, "Why, Lord?" It would have been so simple to say, *"Yes, Lord, we will do it."* However, as before, we had allowed our spiritual thoughts, actions and prayers to become stagnant. One more time, instead of placing God first, the daily activities and routines began to take priority.

Once again, *we discovered that we were about to get the shock of our lives.* The next message from the Lord shook us clear to the core of our foundation.

October 18–**"My children, these are My words"**

"Why do you say you don't know 'why' you are on this journey? YOU DON'T KNOW WHY? If you don't know why by now, you haven't learned anything! I advise you to go back over everything again. See 'WHY' you started this journey and find out the answers to 'WHY.' If you don't understand then, we will stop right now and the journey will be over! You will go on with your lives as before... no difference —-no smarter—-no wiser. I will leave you and go no further. I will use others who will be the least likely in your eyes. So, what will it be? You need to get together and figure this out, before it is too late! Do you hear Me?" God

Why Did We Worry?

These harsh, intense words gave us choices to either move ahead, or quit the journey. *We had to make a decision.* At that point, there was a major concern that we might be running out of our last opportunities to make things right. It made us very nervous and unsettled. It was humbling to know that God was STILL giving us another chance to get back on track, in spite of our lack of obedience.

October 18–**"My children, these are My words"**

"All of these parts of the body have a different function, not only in the body, but in My Spirit, and in My work that I have for you. They each represent how you are to live a clean life. After the last day of praying for the parts of the body, you are to find the one meaning for each part that means the most to you, and you will use that to pray for others.

"It will also teach you how to pray for yourselves when you struggle with your own infirmities.

"All of these lessons are for reasons and solutions. You will understand My words. When you finish the puzzle, all the pieces will be put together and you will understand why you are on this journey. You are to be of one mind...Mine!

"Be in one accord! Stay together and understand! I am here to help and humble you." Your loving Father, God

We received more words from the Lord. **"There is great difficulty coming, 'GREAT DIFFICULTY.' Be prepared! You will need food, fuel and provisions. Pray for the Body of Christ, My people. Many will fall away, but many will come to Me. Be prepared!"**

The next evening during our quiet time, the Lord spoke to us about the journey through the body.

October 19 - **"My children, these are My words"**
"What is the purpose of the trip through the body, you ask? It is so you will have the mind, thoughts and heart for the Body of Christ. You will recall what you have learned when it is needed. There will be successes and failures. The failures will not be your fault. People have choices! There will be dangers, but not physical dangers. You will use what you have learned. Some will be helped, and some will fall through the cracks. You will do well. You may stumble from time to time, but that is all right. David stumbled, as did Moses, along with many of My sons and daughters. Stay on course. We will talk more at a later time."

We were told to wrap the words that we had written about our worries around the third stone and throw the stone into a dumpster that did not belong to us. We all chose dumpsters that were located in areas other than our own property. We were apprehensive about throwing the stones in the dumpsters. (The concern was that someone would find the words.)

One of the dumpsters was located behind a commercial building. Nearby was a large, green dumpster, which was empty except for two open-ended boxes. One of us threw the "worry rock" at the box, but it missed and landed on the floor of the empty dumpster. A prayer asking the Lord if it was all right to leave it there resulted in no answer. After receiving no answer, the individual turned around to go back to the car. Looking down, the individual received the answer to the prayer. On the ground, in plain sight, was a worn out penny with the words IN GOD WE TRUST. This was confirmation that it was all right to leave the rock where it fell in the dumpster. It was also affirmation that this little prayer was not insignificant to God. This was a gentle reminder that God hears all prayers and answers even the smallest requests in His perfect timing. The Lord was definitely aware of our concerns, and revealed that the words would deteriorate in the landfill.

> *Finally, be strong in the Lord and in his mighty power. Put on the full armor of God so that you can take your stand against the devil's schemes. For our struggle is not against flesh and blood, but against the rulers, against the authorities, against the powers of this dark world and against*

> *the spiritual forces of evil in the heavenly realms. Therefore put on the full armor of God, so that when the day of evil comes, you may be able to stand your ground, and after you have done everything, to stand. Stand firm then, with the belt of truth buckled around your waist, with the breastplate of righteousness in place, and with your feet fitted with the readiness that comes from the gospel of peace. In addition to all this, take up the shield of faith, with which you can extinguish all the flaming arrows of the evil one. Take the helmet of salvation and the sword of the Spirit, which is the word of God. And pray in the Spirit on all occasions with all kinds of prayers and requests. With this in mind, be alert and always keep on praying for all the saints.*
> *Ephesians 6:10-18 (NIV)*

Throwing the third stone symbolized the release of fears, worries, concerns, and doubts.
This was our third battle/Goliath.

In His infinite wisdom, the Lord knew that we needed to get refocused on our journey. God blessed us with three days of rest and recuperation. Those days were spent gratefully praising Him for allowing us the time to quietly reflect on how we were going to honor God's requests in the future.

October 25- **"My children, these are My words"**
"Take time for yourselves and rest. You have done well. As you rest, there will be opportunity to lift My name up to others. DO SO! Enjoy some free time, but don't forget Me during those days.

Worship Me however you want, but WORSHIP ME! There is more ahead that I need you to do, but for now, rest these days."

There was a strong sense that this assignment was to teach us new ways to support, love on, and encourage members of the Body of Christ. One of the many ways we were taught was through another vision, accompanied by the interpretation.

<u>VISION</u>: We were shown grayish/tan quicksand swirling around in a pit. Someone was in the middle of it and was sinking into the quicksand until only their head was showing. They were screaming for help, and no one was there to hear or save them.

<u>INTERPRETATION</u>: We must be strong, ready, willing emotionally, physically and spiritually, to hear and support those who are helpless, hopeless and in despair.

As you read this, our prayer is that you will comprehend, as we did, that God will do what He says, and use whom He chooses. Therefore, be wise and obey the first time you are called. God's mission WILL be accomplished, whether you do the task, or someone else is chosen. There are always those waiting in line who are willing to finish a job that God called you to complete.

THE LORD KEEPS HIS PROMISES,
AND ALWAYS DOES WHAT HE SAYS

ASSIGNMENT 8

SPEAKING TO ONE A DAY

ONE A DAY

I will search for my lost ones who strayed away, and I will bring them safely home again...
Ezekiel 34:16 (NLT)

SPEAKING TO ONE A DAY

> *But how can they call on him to save them unless they believe in him? And how can they believe in him if they have never heard about him? And how can they hear about him unless someone tells them? And how will anyone go and tell them without being sent...? Romans 10:14-15 (NLT)*

As we traveled the path the Lord prepared for us along our journey, we were constantly amazed at the way God orchestrated each of our days. He reminded us many times that He was, and is, and will always be in charge of time. We were called to go on a thirty-day journey with the Lord, assuming it would be thirty calendar days. Once again, we tried to wrap our minds around the mystery of God's perfect timing. According to our calendar, we were on day 219 of this journey. God's time frame indicated we were only on day twenty-one of His thirty-day journey with us. We were reminded of the scripture we had been given at the beginning of the book.

> *But you must not forget this one thing, dear friends: A day is like a thousand years to the Lord, and a thousand years is like a day.*
> 2 Peter 3:8 (NLT)

We had been abundantly blessed with restful days to worship and praise the Lord. The quiet days gave us time to reflect on the awesome ways that we had learned (many times through trial and error) about God's unconditional love for mankind. Now, it was time for us to move forward with a new sense of anticipation and hope, and put it into practice.

October 26–**"My children, these are My words"**

"When you speak with others, be bold, but not over-bearing. People are tired of 'Christianity People.' Speak with a gentle spirit and do not be wise in your own eyes.

"Record your experience with each person. Record My words that I have given to you. Be as I have been. I will give the words, but you must also be a good listener. Consider the fact that others may need Me, but are afraid to speak about it.

"Don't forget the children. Talk with them about Me. It will leave My love in their hearts when they have no one else. Try to have a conversation of why I love them, not just saying 'Jesus loves you.' Children and adults love stories. Remember My stories and tell them.

"The entire journey that you are on is not only to help you grow, but to help your understanding on different levels. You will need different meanings, so that you will be able to show and tell any age, at any time.

"Walk carefully, and not in your own shoes. Let My mind and heart show through yours. It is an important time in your lives. Make Me proud! Fill your hearts with so much love that others will truly know and feel it. See and look at their hearts first, then you will know what to pray for them.

"You may see surprises and hear many wonderful stories yourselves. Be alert and pay attention to others. Guard your mouths. Keep your tone low. Be alert, but humble. Remember, you will pray with one person a day, for six days. Make that one person count in both of your lives. This is for you more than the one with whom you speak. Make it count! Make it last within your minds! Make it a pleasure for the other person! Let it be well done for Me!"

Each of us experienced different reactions from the individuals with whom we spoke. Not every individual was receptive to our conversations.

We encountered people who came from many different walks of life. They included, but were not limited to: Children, Homeless Person, Gideon Representative, Teacher, Retail Clerk, Stroke Victim, Dentist, Computer Technician, Student, Grandchildren, Inebriated Individual. The following are seven of many positive responses from those individuals:

One person was concerned about health issues for a family member. After a lengthy conversation and prayer, the person felt confident that God was watching over and holding their loved one in the palm of His hand.

One of us spoke with a young couple with two teenage young adults. They confessed that they had a tendency, as parents, to move ahead of God, by controlling their children's everyday decisions and time management. The parents realized that they needed to rely on God's promises to watch over their children. They were willing to make positive changes, by allowing their teenagers the freedom to be more independent.

During an insightful discussion, a young high school student related that they were very aware of and understood the importance of God remaining in the center of all teen values and morals.

There was another conversation with a grandchild who attended school with several friends who had different religious beliefs and cultures. This high school student was very concerned for them, because she was totally aware that there is only one True God. It was encouraging to know that this student was willing to step out in faith, to speak of God who created the world, and loves everyone, even if they did not know Him.

Another response was as follows: One cold, brisk October day, while walking along the river in Savannah, a woman was observed making beautiful crosses from palm branches. Walking past her, she asked if she could sell one of them to me. As the conversation continued, the woman unfolded her incredible story. One year earlier, her home in another state had been washed away by a flood. She had nothing left, no job, and no family with whom she could stay. With the belongings that she managed to salvage, she made her way to Savannah, where she lived on the streets. One day she met someone who had also been living on the streets. The person taught her how to make crosses out of palms, and she began selling them in a different location. Each time she collected enough money from the sale of the crosses, she would use it to pay for a room at a cheap hotel, for one night. While there, she could enjoy a shower with clean, running water to bathe, and a comfortable bed in which to sleep. The next day, she would return to living on the streets.

She related how she loved the Lord and knew He would take care of her, no matter how the circumstances unfolded. She stated that she knew God personally and was very confident that she would be fine. Her warmth and infectious smile exploded from within her the entire time she talked about the Lord.

As the conversation came to an end, it was very apparent that this beautiful woman was one of God's ambassadors, by showing His love on the streets of Savannah. There was such a lesson to learn from her. She was, in her own simple way of life, affirming to others that there is always hope for the future, as long as one carries that hope of the Lord in one's heart.

As my return trip approached, there was a security of knowing that there would be a warm, comfortable home awaiting me. A feeling of sadness flooded my thoughts. If everything familiar was taken away, would the belief stay strong in knowing the Lord would protect and take care of me in all circumstances? Reflecting on the conversation with the homeless woman, there was a realization that the woman had the love of the Lord, and therefore, had everything she needed. There was a radiant peace about her that resulted from having that inner strength.

Another one of us related the following: Going to the gym three times a week was part of my regular routine. Each day, while riding the exercise bike, a polite, reserved, gentleman would also be riding the exercise bike adjacent to it. It was very apparent that he struggled to complete his exercises for the day. He rarely spoke, but politely acknowledged each smile that was shown to him by others.

In His infinite wisdom (and sense of humor), God used two unlikely, but beautiful, examples of His creation to allow the two of us to strike up our first conversation. As we sat on our exercise bikes, we both laughed as we observed two little crows pecking at their reflections in the glass window that was right in front of us. Who would have thought that two black crows would be the "ice breaker" for conversations that would ultimately show the love of Christ by glorifying His holy name?

Upon engaging in conversation with the gentleman, it was learned that he was exercising in an attempt to recover from a stroke. For a few days we engaged in general conversations about our families and our jobs. Soon, there was a beautiful transformation in the man's countenance. His sense of humor, wit, charm, and gentle spirit began to surface and bloom, just like a flower coming through the hard ground on a warm spring day. *His actions were like a breath of fresh air.* His demeanor dictated joy, compassion, peace and most of all love, to all those he encountered.

This man stated that he knew for a fact that God's mercy and grace had saved his life. As a result of the stroke, his emotions were very vulnerable, which made him apprehensive to talk about what the Lord had done for him. He was eager to learn more about Jesus, but these extenuating circumstances held him back from asking questions. As the days went by, we became more comfortable talking about the Lord. The flavor of his conversations was always very creative and positive. There was never a day that he spoke negative words about his unhealthy circumstances. It was very apparent that he was keeping room in his heart for the Lord. He definitely gave the unconditional sincerity of his heart to others. The invaluable lessons learned from this incredible man will be embedded in this heart for a lifetime. Others may outwardly appear to have their "act together," but their inner feelings could be crying out for someone to understand their struggles.

Unfortunately, there were also negative responses. Some were indifferent about what was being spoken. Others lacked the desire to listen or learn about the Lord at that particular time. We sensed that God was asking us to engage in many future opportunities to speak with others about the Lord. Learning from those with whom we spoke encouraged us to have a sensitivity to accept them where they were on their own personal walk.

October 27- We were instructed to spend the entire day praying for God's animals, birds, insects, reptiles, and species of the waters.

It was exciting to devote an entire day praying for all of God's creatures. Sometimes God's creatures are our best teaching tools. It continually warms the heart to see how their parenting skills show love and tenderness for their young. When it comes to fierce protection of their offspring, nothing is off limits to secure their safety. God created His creatures to have survival mechanisms, intense instincts to detect friend or foe, parenting skills, respect, plus the ability to sense sorrow, pain, joy, and most of all love. One doesn't have to wonder about their credibility. All their behaviors are uniquely genuine, because God created them this way. If we would consciously observe God's creatures, there may be a lesson for each of us in every move they make.

Once again, God chose to give us another teaching/learning tool, by revealing a vision and interpretation for us to file away in our spirits.

VISION: We were shown faces of the following creatures: horse, dog, cat, frog, reptile, monkey, alligator, and birds. (These represented samples of all God's creatures that He had created.) He directed us to pray for the following: protection, health, food, shelter, reproduction, and love. The Lord said, **"I created them the same as I did you."**

INTERPRETATION: God is saying that we can learn from the animals. They have wisdom of their own (nature and habits specifically). God's creatures are definitely masters at teaching us about unconditional love. They must also rely on God's provisions. Why don't we "rely" on God's resources?

> *"Just ask the animals, and they will teach you. Ask the birds of the sky, and they will tell you. Speak to the earth, and it will instruct you. Let the fish in the sea speak to you." Job 12:7-8 (NLT)*

> *And God said, "Let the earth produce every sort of animal, each producing offspring of the same kind – livestock, small animals that scurry along the ground, and wild animals." And that is what happened. Genesis 1:24 (NLT)*

> *"The wild animals honor me, the jackals and the owls, because I provide water in the desert and streams in the wasteland"...Isaiah 43:20 (NIV)*

November 2–**"My children, these are My words"**

"My three devoted children. In spite of the daily chores and activities, you have still been faithful to Me. These past six days have been eye-opening, as to how freely you were able to discuss My Name. You saw how there are others who

wanted and needed to discuss and learn about Me and My goodness. Some were not responsive and had a tendency to hold others back, which may have made them apprehensive and/or afraid. Don't worry about that. On a daily basis, continue to spread My life, My name, and our light. Others do receive it no matter how you show it. Remember, you are to shine your light and show others the way, until I come back for them to see for themselves. Sometimes, it will feel like John, where others wanted to put his head on a silver platter, just to shut his mouth. However, as my prophets and dear children, continue no matter what type of reaction you receive.

"Become who I need you to become, so that you can go out and do My work. May each of you find peace, comfort and direction that will allow you to have a better understanding of yourself. I am here teaching you daily. Continue to walk in My light." Your Heavenly Father

God is always beginning something new every day. If we are growing in the Lord, that means we cannot stay the same as we were yesterday. We are called to not only be hearers of the word, but doers as well. Our job is not to "fix and heal," but to become beacons of light in the midst of darkness. When God plants an idea in your mind to accomplish something for Him, trust that the Holy Spirit will allow others to receive it when shared. The Lord can, and will, work through us when we surrender our will to His.

DO NOT BE WISE IN YOUR OWN EYES

ASSIGNMENT 9

IDENTIFYING WITH THE PROPHETS

THE PROPHETS

You must warn each other every day, while it is still "today," so that none of you will be deceived by sin and hardened against God.
Hebrews 3:13 (NLT)

IDENTIFYING WITH THE PROPHETS

"I will raise up a prophet like you from among their fellow Israelites. I will put my words in his mouth, and he will tell the people everything I command him. I will personally deal with anyone who will not listen to the messages the prophet proclaims on my behalf." Deuteronomy 18:18-19 (NLT)

There were times when we were in the middle of one journey, that the Lord gave us instructions for the next journey. This part of the journey was a history lesson about prophets from past times. From them, we would be learning how to apply those lessons to current times.

October 29–**"My children, these are My words"**

"Children, I want you to learn right from wrong, past and present. Situations are always the same, only in different eras. This era is just as corrupt as the others. People still turn away from Me.

People still rob, cheat and steal. Identities are still not allowed to be kept quiet. There are and were fights, land stealing, corrupt people. It is still the same! I am still the same. My messages then are the same now. There are different people, the same countries, known by different names. We must do now what I did before, and learn all over again, what I told the prophets and people before this era.

"You will need to carry the mantle of My past prophets. You won't know how to do this unless you learn about them. Now I will teach you what I taught them and see if you can relate to any of them. "Our next journey is to learn from each one of the prophets. As you read, there will be questions from each prophet that you will answer. These are the questions:

"Do you feel like this one prophet?

"Would you like to become more like this prophet?

"Do you identify with this one prophet?

"Do you feel their burdens?

"Do you feel led to walk down his same path?

"Do you act like this prophet?

"Have you been where this prophet has been?

"What words would you use to tell others about each prophet's situation in our time, our day, and what will happen if we don't?

"Children, through this journey we have been on you have learned a great many things: fear, time, curses, blessings, what happens with disobedience, what our results are with corrections, times of pain, sorrow, and happiness. You are learning much about yourselves and others. Now you will learn and practice different ways to pray for healing. There will be no other messengers such as you. Each and everyone else I choose, will be for a different purpose and meaning. In reality it is always about Me, and the different ways and means of My works.

"This will be the beginning of another journey of learning. Each one now should be exciting and fulfilling. You need only to continue to say yes, as you have previously done. We can't turn back now. You are desperately needed. I have much more to teach and there is so much you must learn. Keep it up. There is much more to do.

"I am with you in mind, Spirit, love and direction. Here we go again to a better life. You will need Me to help others stand firm, stand tall, stand up for Me, and stay on My track, the track leading to the highway of heaven.

"My love and thanks." Your Father in Heaven

For the next fourteen days, we were instructed to read about and learn from the Old Testament prophets listed below. It was astonishing to learn of the many times the prophets boldly conveyed painful, yet persevering, truthful messages to the unconcerned, unbelieving people of their times. It must have been difficult for those prophets to consistently and obediently proclaim the truth and promises of God. In spite of the confrontations by those who laughed at and mocked them the prophets remained faithful. Knowing they were not always in a welcoming setting, they shamelessly spoke the truthful words of the Lord. Many profound lessons can be gleaned from the Old Testament prophets.

The Lord has also chosen people of our day to be His servants, the prophets. Warnings of sin and judgment apply to people today, just as they did in biblical times. The main things God wants from all of us are to listen and be obedient. It remains our choice, as to how we respond to these modern day messengers.

> *Indeed, the Sovereign Lord never does anything until he reveals his plans to his servants the prophets. Amos 3:7 (NLT)*

As we began our research and study of the prophets, we learned that the "office" of prophet began during the days of Samuel, the last of the judges. A prophet's role was to stand with the priests as God's special representative. He spoke for God as he confronted the people and their leaders with God's commands and

Identifying With The Prophets

promises. True prophets usually were not very popular, because of the confrontations and tendencies of people to disobey God. A prophet's message often went unheeded, but they faithfully and forcefully proclaimed the truth.

All three of us had the same thought-provoking reaction. Would we feel very comfortable standing before a disorderly, hostile crowd, boldly and confidently witnessing about God's unending, unconditional love for mankind?

It was interesting to note that a title (special meaning) was assigned to each prophet's name. Their names are recorded in the Spirit-Filled Life Bible (NKJV) – New King James Version.

You will see the name "Yahweh" in the following prophets' names, which means "I AM."

ISAIAH: "Yahweh Is Salvation"
Isaiah called the people to a special relationship with God, although judgment through other nations was inevitable. Sometimes we must suffer judgment and discipline before we are restored to God.

Knowing that time is growing shorter, God is asking us to turn away from our pleasure seeking and return to Him. Working to have a deeper relationship with God allows Him to be first in our lives. Searching the scriptures for clarity and truth enables us to find peace in our everyday life.

It was hard for us to identify with the prophet Isaiah, because we lacked discipline, obedience, and initiative to be encouragers. However, our goal is to become faithful and obedient to witness to others without judgment. When God asks "Whom shall I send?" (*6:8*), we would like to be one of the many to answer the call.

JEREMIAH: "Yahweh Exalts" and "Yahweh Throws"

Even though Jeremiah was younger than twenty years of age, God still used him to boldly speak of repentance, judgment, the fall of nations, and punishment. He also received many visions from the Lord. It should also be noted that Jeremiah is the longest book in the Bible.(based on the original language)

Just as Jeremiah spoke, we too, should try to tell others about the Lord. Even at a young age, one can be a prophet, but we need to be gentle and wise when we witness. There are those who are weak in spirit and tend not to listen. If we turn our lives over to the Lord, He will protect, guide, and guard us from the secular world, in which many choose to live. We found that one of the most encouraging verses in the book of Jeremiah tells of God's plans and promises for us. (*Jeremiah 29:11*)

Identifying With The Prophets

LAMENTATIONS: The author was not named, but traditions claim Jeremiah wrote it. As was their custom, the Jewish people used the first word of the book as its title, and it originally became known as "Ekah," "How."

This book teaches people that to disobey God is to invite disaster, and to show that God also suffers when His people suffer.

Lamentations is a book of tears, deep sorrow, poems and a prayer for mercy. It teaches how to express sorrow without losing hope. There is hope and redemption when we return to the Lord, but there are also consequences and suffering if we stray. Don't rebel against God's authority. Listen to those who are wise, experienced and knowledgeable about the prophets/God's words. Only God knows the heart of man. We are called to be encouragers of the Word.

EZEKIEL: "God Strengthens"

When the Lord spoke to Ezekiel he referenced him as "Son of man." Ezekiel sent messages back to Jerusalem, urging the people to turn back to God before they were all forced to join him in exile. After Jerusalem fell, he urged his fellow exiles to turn back to God, so they could eventually return to their homeland. God disciplines His people to draw them closer to Him.

We cannot excuse ourselves from our responsibilities before God. We are accountable to Him for our choices. The consequences of our actions can be rewarding or devastating. It depends on if we do or don't turn back to God and repent. As a country, we must be aware that God will restore our nation when, and only when, we repent. *Ezekiel 3:17-19* states that it is our responsibility to warn people about God's judgment and His message of salvation, but if they choose not to listen, we are not held accountable.

DANIEL: "God Is My Judge"

Daniel described both near and distant future events. Through it all, God is sovereign and triumphant. We should spend less time wondering when the events will happen, and more time learning how we should live now. This would keep us from being victims of those circumstances.

Daniel spoke frequently about end times, the anti-Christ, and future events. God made a covenant with His people Israel, and said that they would be His people and He would be their God. It is impossible to be a part of that covenant without repenting and turning to God. When we humble ourselves before God and pay attention to His covenant, our words are heard.

HOSEA: "Salvation or Deliverance"

Hosea condemned the people of Israel because they had sinned against God, as an adulterous woman sins against her husband. When we sin, we sever our relationship to God, which breaks our commitment to Him. While all must answer to God for their sins, those who seek God's forgiveness are spared from eternal judgment.

We have turned away from God as individuals and as a nation. Our commitment of loyalty, obedience, and faithfulness in honoring God has been broken. Forgiveness and restoration can be ours if we release those burdens back to Him. God's love knows no bounds.

JOEL: "Yahweh Is God"

Because a plague of locusts had come to punish the nation, Joel called the people to turn back to God before an even greater judgment occurred. While God judges all people for their sins, He gives eternal salvation to those who have turned to Him.

God is revealing many signs and wonders, such as many natural disasters; i.e., fires, floods, famines, droughts, crop failures, and earthquakes. From these disasters, we learn that God brings rain on the just and unjust alike. Both will suffer equally during these times. Those who turn back, repent, follow, obey and worship God alone will be granted His mercies and entrance into His Heavenly Kingdom. In doing this, there is that beautiful promise of eternal life for each of us. Remember also that God is gracious, slow to anger, compassionate, and abounding in loving kindness. (Joel *2:13*)

AMOS: "Burden Bearer"

Amos warned those who exploited or ignored the needy. Believing in God is more than a personal matter. God calls all believers to work against injustice in society, and to aid those less fortunate.

Everyone is held accountable to God. Often times, blessings are taken for granted. He promises restoration to those who are willing to be obedient in integrity, truth, honor, finances, and carefully weighing our words as we respectfully speak to others. There is an obligation to help correct injustice, and assist our brothers and sisters. God is judging, and bringing to justice, those who have turned their backs on Him. Judgment brings revenge to the prideful ones. The challenge to each of us is to take the time and energy to encourage a healthy relationship with one another.

OBADIAH: "Servant/Worshiper of Yahweh"

God judged the Edomites for taking advantage of God's people. Pride is one of the most dangerous sins, because it causes us to take advantage of others.

Our Heavenly Father responds with judgment to all who would attack those whom He loves. Judgment will be brought about to those who are in defiance of God. Whether we are the fortunate, or less fortunate, we must never forget that we are all God's children.

He requires us to treat each other with respect. As you have done, it will be done to you... (*v. 15*)

JONAH: "Dove" or "Pigeon"

Jonah was asked by God to warn the people of Nineveh, but refused and ran the other direction. After being severely disciplined by the Lord, he did warn Nineveh, the capital of Assyria, to repent of its sins. God wants all nations to turn to Him. His love reaches out to all peoples.

God does not want us to avoid His message, as His words are for everyone. We must not be concerned for our own reputation, because He works everything for good. There are consequences for those who rebel and run from God. We should realize that God may want to use you as His personal instrument to accomplish the message of His sovereignty and compassion.

MICAH: Name predicates a Likeness to the Lord. "He Who Is Like Yahweh."

Micah predicted the fall of both the northern and southern kingdoms. This was God's discipline on the people, which actually showed how much He cared for them. Choosing to live a life apart from God is making a commitment to sin. Sin leads to judgment and death. God alone shows us the way to eternal peace. His discipline often keeps us on the right path.

We learned that God mysteriously reveals Himself in many different ways. He is commanding us to do what is right, to love mercy, and to walk humbly with Him. (6:8) The Almighty Lord hates a sin and loves the sinner. Micah represents the true picture of God.

NAHUM: "Comforter or Full of Comfort"

Nineveh, the mighty empire of Assyria that oppressed God's people, would soon tumble. It was a city of disobedience, rebellion, injustice, cruelty and despair. Those who do evil and oppress others will one day meet a bitter end.

Those who get ahead by deception will one day find out that there is a point of no return. God never changes! *He is the same yesterday, today, and forever. (Hebrews 13:8)*

HABAKKUK: "Embrace"

Habakkuk couldn't understand why God seemed to do nothing about the wickedness in society. Eventually, he realized that faith in God alone would one day supply the answer.

God always answers our questions. Sometimes the answers may be "Yes." Others may be "No," and often times the answer is "Not Yet." (3:16)

We can rest assured that even though judgment may not come quickly, justice will be served in His perfect timing. His ways are everlasting.

ZEPHANIAH: "The Lord Has Hidden"

A day would come when God, as judge, would intensely punish all nations; but afterward He would show mercy to His people. We will all be judged for our disobedience to God, but if we remain faithful to Him, He will show us mercy.

It was obvious to us, this prophet told of political and social issues contrary to God, which is much like our country today. God will bring justice to those who stray from His words. Those who stand firm in the Lord will survive. We should listen and accept His corrections and move toward the Lord.

A nation will never become so powerful that God can't bring them down. *What the Lord wants done, it shall be done.* Remove from the minds of man their individualism. May we all be numbered in the Body of Christ, Church Triumphant. We are moving, one day at a time, to a grand appointment. Will we be ready?

HAGGAI: "Festive"

Haggai called the people to complete the rebuilding of the temple that had been previously destroyed.

Listening for God to speak to us is essential. He needs His time of worship with us so that we can receive His encouragement. At times, priorities get mixed up and there is a tendency to neglect the temple (the Church). By having a strong reverence for the Lord, attitudes can change. *Make God your first priority.* He wants to change the world through us, His ambassadors.

ZECHARIAH: "Yahweh Remembers"

Zechariah was called to give hope to God's people by revealing God's future deliverance through the Messiah. He was a man who received many of the Lord's messages by means of visions.

Zechariah had strong, encouraging words for the people. We, too, can honor God by witnessing and telling others how much God loves us and controls our future. There is hope and peace for those who trust in His Mighty Name.

MALACHI: "My Messenger"

Malachi was the last prophet and the last book of the Old Testament. He predicted the fall of both the Northern and Southern kingdoms. This was God's discipline on the people, which actually showed how much He cared for them.

We learned that we need to honor God with our service and our tithes. How we live reflects the sincerity of our love for Him. Our life is God's gift to us.

He is a jealous God. He wants our full attention, and for us to make Him our first priority.

There is much to learn, because we inherit our present from stories of the past. Just as the prophets in the Bible spoke to crowds, we, too, can learn from them. Their boldness to speak was God-given, even in spite of negative responses. The faithfulness that they inherited may be an inspiration for us to begin our own "witnessing walk" as a spokesperson to tell others about God's unconditional love for them.

November 11–**"My children, these are My words"**

"Child – Of these times, what makes you nervous or uneasy? In the days of Joseph, was there not a time of famine with him? What percent of their income was dedicated to a food storehouse? They were told to be ready. What about now? Do you feel that you need a food supply? I gave them, and am giving to my prophets now, specific words and directions.

"There will be a day of sadness, despair and wonders. Even though the skies will be a rich blue in color, there will be darkness in hearts. There will be days where people will not know which direction to turn. Some will turn to Me, others to their own gods. Others will rely solely on themselves. Some will run in circles and others will just run with no place to go.

"If I told you I wanted you to have food stored for two weeks, would you do that without questions? If I told you to collect food for two months, would you listen? If I told you to prepare and collect food for two years, would you be skeptical? How much do you trust my words and assignments?

"Children, how much do you believe I am speaking and warning you and others? There are so many who are lost. Be kind and generous to them. Do what you have to do, in My Name, so later you will be witnesses to My promises and words. You will know and see that I am the God of all supplies, health and circumstances.

"Many sit and react better to darkness. Then they won't have to shine their light and take care of others. Are you afraid of days ahead, and what may happen? I will provide for and comfort you. My children, do as I ask and know that I am here for you, and will never leave. Do not be afraid!

"You are learning from My prophets how to listen, be better equipped, what to stay away from, and what I need you to say and do. Don't be afraid of what others say or do to you! Don't get overwhelmed! Be smart! I know exactly who will listen, which ones will run and hide, and who will have sorrow later. You need to know how to be smart and listen to Me and to each other. When the time is right, you will be blessed and be a blessing. For now, depend on each other, with My words and prophecies to each of you. Be smart, be aware, but don't be ashamed or frightened. Live life as it should be lived, renewed and restored. Listen to truth–ME!"

During the next eight days, we studied the prophets' actions and responses, to see how the past prophets could impact our current lives, as we spoke to people about the Lord.

November 19–**"My children, these are My words"**
"You will need to finish My prophets so you will learn both of their struggles and how they got out of them. There is much you can still learn from them.

"You will cast your fourth stone shortly, and then you will pray for three days. We need closure on this subject. You knew it would get more difficult.

"Listen to the prophets. Understand the prophets and do as they did. This is why you are reading them.

"Go in My Name, not yours. Go in peace, not anger. Go in joy, not hatred. Do My work as I asked. I am here with you every step of the way.

Pay attention and be wise! I speak, you listen and do."

A loving Father interceding for you in love.

Choosing to live a life of sin is like making a commitment to walk away from God. Sin is like being allergic to the love of God. He is very willing to forgive if we ask...no matter what we have done. Injections of grace can be painful when asking for forgiveness for those things that break His heart. He is asking us to have the passion to be a spokesman and mouthpiece for Him. We can experience this passion by making a commitment to love, honor and obey the Lord in all that we do and say.

THE LORD REIGNS THE SAME
YESTERDAY, TODAY, AND FOREVER

ASSIGNMENT 10

PROCRASTINATION TO DISOBEDIENCE

TWELVE STONE MEMORIAL

Now what I am commanding you today is not too difficult for you or beyond your reach. Deuteronomy 30:11 (NIV)

PROCRASTINATION TO DISOBEDIENCE

When the whole nation had finished crossing the Jordan, the Lord said to Joshua, "Choose twelve men from among the people, one from each tribe, and tell them to take up twelve stones from the middle of the Jordan from right where the priests stood and to carry them over with you and put them down at the place where you stay tonight." So Joshua called together the twelve men he had appointed from the Israelites, one from each tribe, and said to them, "Go over before the ark of the Lord your God into the middle of the Jordan. Each of you is to take up a stone on his shoulder, according to the number of the tribes of the Israelites, to serve as a sign among you. In the future, when your children ask you, 'What do these stones mean?' Tell them that the flow of the Jordan was cut off before the ark of the covenant of the Lord. When it crossed the Jordan, the waters of the Jordan were cut off. These stones are to be a memorial to the people of Israel forever." So the Israelites did as Joshua commanded them. They took twelve stones from the middle of the Jordan, according to the number of the tribes of the Israelites, as the Lord had told Joshua; and they carried them over with them to their camp, where they put them down. Joshua set up the

> twelve stones that had been in the middle of the Jordan at the spot where the priests who carried the Ark of the Covenant had stood. And they are there to this day. Joshua 4:1-9 (NIV)

We were beginning to clearly recognize a new and different phase of our journey with the Lord. It constantly amazed us that we could be walking a different path, in addition to the journey that we were currently experiencing. *God is just amazing.*

November 19–**"My children, these are My words"**

"Cast your fourth stone and then pray for three more days. We need closure on this subject. You knew it would get more difficult."

When we allowed our hearts and minds to capture the powerful ways that God works in each of us, we were humbled again and again. We were often neglectful of our time management and quiet times with the Lord. We sensed a new awareness that our journey could be more exhilarating and positive, if we would concentrate on God's plan for us each day, instead of questioning the unknown plans ahead of us.

The entire four days that we remained in prayer about all of the things that caused us to react in a negative manner, we asked for God's forgiveness and mercy. The Lord told us to search our hearts and confess anything that was offensive to God. When we became truthful with ourselves, we realized that our burdens were very heavy and unattractive to think about, let alone confess.

Then came our new instructions. The Lord instructed us to take a piece of paper and make a list of all the things that were unsettling to us in every facet of our lives. This subject was stressful, because the list of concerns began to expand and overwhelmingly multiply. By writing down all of the troublesome issues, we realized that we had been carrying "baggage" that should have been purged years ago. When discussing our lists, it became very apparent that the three of us carried some of the same baggage. There were common denominators, as our thoughts drifted toward our church, families, finances, medical, friends, and attitudes. Everyday living sometimes causes "bumps in the road." Unexpected obstacles and circumstances had cluttered our path, and we were not focusing on the guidelines that the Lord laid out for us. Personal feelings had taken precedent over God's agenda. Viewing our list helped us to understand that we had made choices that constituted taking a fork in the road that was not pleasing to the Lord.

Search me, O God, and know my heart; test me and know my anxious thoughts. Point out anything in me that offends you, and lead me along the path of everlasting life. Psalm 139:23-24 (NLT)

November 25–"**My children, these are My words**"

"**You are My spokespersons. Don't put your personal feelings ahead of My agenda. You can do better than that. Do what I have told you. Pray from your heart! Don't judge! Don't worry about time. You know about My time. Don't pray in anger. I need all of your prayers in love and sincerity.**"

If you remember reading earlier in this book, the Lord directed us to collect five stones, which would be symbolic of the fact that we would face five Goliaths/battles on our journey. We were about to throw our fourth stone. Not understanding what this meant for us, we had to quiet our spirits and listen for directions. God's plan remains a mystery until He is ready to reveal it, and it will then be His perfect timing. At this exact point in time, He revealed specific instructions to us.

The three of us were instructed to take the piece of paper on which we had written all of our unsettled situations, and wrap it around the fourth stone. After completing that, the final step was to bury our individual stones on the property where we lived. Then we were to collect twelve stones and place them on top of that place where we buried our fourth stone. As a symbolic covenant with the Lord, this act was to remind us that we released (gave up) those things that seemed to be a weight/burden on us. We knew that we had to let go of the past and look forward to a bright and positive future. When we looked at that site where we placed the stones, it would confirm to us that God had taken all of those burdens from us, never to be remembered again.

Each of us prayed over our list of concerns, and as instructed, wrapped the paper around the fourth stone and buried it in a specific location on the property, which could be seen at any given time. The symbolic monument of twelve stones was a constant reminder that we had conquered the giant/battle that had previously kept us from being confident and powerful witnesses for God's kingdom.

December 1–**"My children, these are My words"**
"Our last stone will not be thrown until you are safe and healed. It (the stone) will be thrown to signify all is completed. We have come to the end of our journey, and this is what you are now to do.
"I want you to explain your journey to a specific individual that I have chosen for you. Tell

this person what you have gone through, not every detail, only what you will be told to say. You will be given words and visions, and you will speak them.

"You will meditate and pray about this meeting and conversation, for the next several days. Then you will come together to get the dates and journey down pat in your minds/spirits.

"Before this meeting, you will need to draw a timeline, with pictures, which will show what you did. You will need the dates, and why you went through it. Speak about each picture and date. Each of you will speak about the part that I have directed you to tell. Do not condemn. Speak only those words that will build up and encourage. This will help to give the person a better understanding of the journey that I have placed you on for several months. Do not let the individual walk away confused about any part of the journey.

"Go in peace and I will be there every step of the way. I love you, My children. Now, let's go all together as one!

"I am All-Knowing! All-Powerful! All-Grateful! This is your chance to put this into power. All you have learned is to be shared. Remember each step and keep yourselves clean. Remember the altar you have made. It will make sense at the end.

"Be careful and call on Me daily. Remember how you prayed, and do it again in unison. Don't go ahead of Me. Don't be proud. I am counting on you to complete the end of My work.

"My messengers, spokespersons, and My children...Do Not Worry! Do not fret! Stay together and we will do it right!

"We all need to be healed. It is up to you to help get it done. Each day, I will be with you to guide you. Don't get ahead of Me and don't rush.

"For now, begin to pray more and harder. You can and will do it." God

Listening to the Lord's words, we were instructed to draw and assemble the chart (timeline) the way we felt it should be done. The pictures drawn would be those that were important to represent our journey. God gave us the freedom to choose and prioritize the timeline. (Later on, we found out that God had something very different in mind.)

> *In his heart a man plans his course, but the Lord determines his steps. Proverbs 16:9 (NIV)*

Even though the deadline was set for us to speak to a designated individual, we procrastinated and claimed we weren't ready to move in that direction. Apprehension and doubt about the outcome prompted every excuse we could think of to delay the assignment.

December 2–**"My children, these are My words"**
The Lord heard and understood our doubts about what He was asking us to do next. He explained to us, **"DON'T DOUBT MY WORDS. HAVE I EVER TAKEN YOU TO PLACES WHERE YOU HAVEN'T BEEN ABLE TO EITHER COPE OR GET OUT?**

"When you enter the meeting, leave a chair for Me and My angel. Do not worry. Be gentle and kind. Do not put your words or extra thoughts into what you have already received. This will not be difficult. There is no time limit on how quickly you finish this assignment. It will be as hard as you make it. If you start to go down the wrong path, I will either shut you down or remove you from this last, long task.

"You have studied, prayed, talked, read, and heard enough words, and have seen enough visions to know better. Complete this and do it right. I will be right beside you, and in the midst of you. It will be done in My behalf. If you have any questions, come to Me and I will answer.

"This journey is more important to Me than it is to you. My children's lives are at stake. You are My messengers to them. In loving kindness, help, save, protect, and nurture My children.

"I AM COUNTING ON YOU. NOW GET PREPARED AND DO MY WORK!" GOD

We knew what God expected of us, but we were unsure of what the response might be. We were very unsettled in our spirits at that time. If we had only known what was about to happen to the three of us. When God tells you to do something, He expects you to do it the first time He asks, or face the consequences.

WE WERE ABOUT TO FACE THE CONSEQUENCES

ASSIGNMENT 11

ALONE IN THE BOAT

THE BOAT

Therefore tell the people: This is what the Lord Almighty says: 'Return to me,' declares the Lord Almighty, 'and I will return to you,' says the Lord Almighty. Zechariah 1:3 (NIV)

ALONE IN THE BOAT

In my distress I called to the Lord; I cried to my God for help. From his temple he heard my voice; my cry came before him, into his ears.
Psalm 18:6 (NIV)

It is noteworthy to mention again that the Lord placed us on a thirty-day journey several months ago. His timing was disclosed to us over and over. We cannot judge God's days by our human thoughts. Here we were, on day twenty-five of our thirty-day journey. It never ceased to amaze us that in the very beginning, we thought we could get through this journey in a very short period of time. Our plan was to walk through it, and just move on. We were shown, day in and day out, that God sees the overall picture of what He wants for our lives. The Lord definitely wanted more from us. It constantly amazed us that He was incredibly patient and willing to walk with us to make it happen.

December 3–Day 25 of 30-day journey

God was taking us to a deeper level in our walk. He was asking us to guard against separation between the Creator and the created. What did that mean and what did that look like for us? The nervousness and unsettling thoughts began to mount, as the three of us read scriptures, and asked for visions and words. He was convicting us that our behavior and actions were again unbecoming of the journey that we had been on for several months. God has a way of bringing attention to our positive and negative actions, and asks us to weigh both, to see where we stand in our walk with Him. Sometimes it is hard to separate the two actions. We can have blinders and deafness on our spiritual eyes and ears, to the extent that what we see and hear is the right decision in our human minds. This was a reaction to our doubt and insecurity. Jesus gives us the authority to use His name. We must rely on His name, knowing that we are His children, and His friends. He gives us the free will to speak out, cry out, and praise His name, with a boldness that can only come from knowing and having a personal relationship with the Lord. It is said that actions speak louder than words. This is true, but they will also echo into the next generation. These were heavy words to carry. Wanting to, and actually making a difference in the lives of the next generation, were two separate thought patterns and actions.

How could we make a difference, especially when the three of us, at times, felt vulnerable and uncertain of ourselves?

December 3–**"My children, these are My words"**
"Thank you for listening to and following My words by speaking the truth. Deliver My words as I tell them. Walk in My truth and don't turn a deaf ear to Me. I'll always be here for you. Cry out to Me and I will answer. Trust and you will be trusted! Love and you will be loved! I am here!" God, Your Father

December 4 – Day 26 of 30-day journey

All day, we cried out to the Lord, praising His name. Each of us fasted from speaking negative thoughts. Prayers were lifted up for clarity, because there was a specific direction the Lord wanted us to take when we created our timeline. (This specific chart/timeline would include pictures, words, scriptures, and days. From this point forward, the chart will read as a timeline.) In the back of our minds, there was a strong sense that our journey was about to take another turn.

December 5 – Day 27 of 30-day journey

Anxiety crept into our thoughts, as we nervously began to draft a timeline of our journey. So much had taken place in our lives, it was hard for us to pinpoint which task or assignment would best relay our message to those needing to hear it. We read scriptures and prayed again for clarity.

December 6 – Day 28 of 30-day journey

We continued to pray about and draft the timeline. Our thirty-day journey was nearing completion. The three of us were having mixed emotions about the journey, because we had not completed our timeline. We were aware that we were to speak to a specific individual before the journey came to a close. Our deadline date was blatantly staring us in the face. (This was part of our procrastination process.) Going back over our journal notes brought reality into the task, and emotions flooded our spirits. It was difficult to decide how it should look, and if we were hearing correctly. This timeline would be critical in helping us to move forward with God's plan for us. God's hand was in this task all along. We all agreed that we needed to be faithful, and there was a thankfulness that God was keeping us on His path, in spite of our lack of discipline and intense procrastination. He provided insight and directions as we drew the timeline.

At the time, we did not comprehend what the Lord was teaching us. This timeline was an example of how God allowed us to have free will in our choices, as to what we felt needed to be included. Again, what we included in the timeline was not necessarily God's choice. (This would not be our last timeline.)

December 6–**"My children, these are My words"**

"My children: Once again, why do you fret? Why are you worried? What makes you think you can't do this? Yes, I know all the things 'you say you have to do.' What about Me? Where do I fit in?

"Your words are for others. I chose the three of you to do one job for the Lord. It was a test of how well you did your job.

"Be wiser in your thoughts. Be wiser in your journey. Do not break the chain now. Do pay attention now. My work needs to be done when I tell you to do it. Stop running away from your last journey. Be careful! You have come so far, and now you are getting off track. STOP!

"When it is easy, you are fine. Pressure doesn't become you. I need your faithfulness now, more than ever. If I don't have it now, it won't be at all. It's up to you...quick and to the point. I don't want others concerned about all of the details. Give them hope and blessings. Don't become righteous. Because I placed you on this journey, be careful. I will let you go in a blink of an eye. What is your decision? Are you ready to finish? If not, and you are too busy, you will be released

from all assignments. I will erase most of it from your minds. It's up to you! What is it that you want to do?

"You take time for Me, and I'll make time for you."

December 7–Day 29 of 30-day journey
As our deadline to speak to the specific individual drew closer, we were grateful for the time to concentrate on praying for wisdom, knowledge and discernment for our meeting.

The next five days were dedicated to prayers of preparation. We asked for clarity, calmness, and peace for each of us. The timeline was now completed and we were ready for the meeting.

December 13 – Day 29 of 30-day journey
The meeting day finally arrived. We met for prayer and read scriptures. However, for varied reasons, the meeting did not take place that day. There were scheduling conflicts with the individual. For the next three days we prayed about the circumstances of our delayed meeting and what we were to do next.

December 16 **"My children, these are My words"**
"The three of you...WHY? Why have you not completed what I have asked you to do? I gave

you ample time and a date for when you were to speak to the individual that I assigned to you. Why did you make your own schedule without asking Me? Why haven't you received visions, dreams, or scriptures from Me in the past week? Why did you do the things I didn't ask or tell you to do? You made time for the things you wanted to do, but not what I asked you to do. I AM ANGRY WITH, AND DISAPPOINTED IN, ALL THREE OF YOU! Yes, I know what the outcome is in all of your journeys. I have told you and shown you before, the results of what will happen, when you do not listen and go your own way. Why did you not complete My small task when I asked you to? Why did you take this task so lightly? I gave you specific dates. I expected them to be done.

"You came to Me in tears and asked for forgiveness. Those were just words from the head, and you have not done correctly with your hearts. Why did you put things and others before Me? Why did you not listen? Why are you making your own time frame from what is to be done here? I gave you the words and you did not complete it as I asked.

"Now, there will be consequences! You can no longer go forward on this assignment. I am placing the three of you (spiritually) in the middle of a desolate boat. There will be no one in it with you to help guide you, feed you the words, or steer you in the right direction. You will be on your own until I come to rescue you. I am disappointed in all three of you. I needed you to complete this task and you took this too lightly. You will feel abandoned for now. All the tears in the world will not help you right now. All the worries and asking for forgiveness will not be heard at this point.

"Beginning today, you will be placed in a very small boat with just enough room for only the three of you. You will be in stormy weather, and feel famine at times. Get into the Word, pray to get scriptures, visions, and words. Pay attention to Me more than ever! I have known throughout this journey that you would complete it. This is the last Goliath/battle, but it will take time to throw the stone. I am sorry to have to do this to you, but you have brought this upon yourselves. When I believe you are ready, I will let you know.

"Now, start reading about all of your disappointments, responsibilities, being disloyal, sadness and brokenness. You three have to get back in touch with one another to become one again. You have been too distant and your prayers have not been sincere. They are the same prayers, day in and day out, with no meanings. We have come far, but for now you will stay distant. Break your schedules for Me. Why have you made other things so much more important than I am? You sit and hear nothing at times, because of My sadness. I am sorry to have to do this, but you still have some learning to do before you can go to others and tell them of My love, devotion, and how much My love really means to them.

"The three of you... Do you understand? I am not only disappointed, but also angry! I am sad! But, through all of this, I still love all three of you. I want you to get this right, to be better witnesses to others. I want others to know there is pain and sadness from both sides (yours and Mine) when you move away from God. Put things back in place where they need to be, and go on. I will be waiting for you, and you will become stronger. Now go and reflect on the mistakes, stay together in prayers that have substance. I will be waiting for you to connect and get where I need you to be. My words will come. Visions are needed. Scriptures will help you read. Get on with My life and yours.

"I pray this Christmas time you will understand to the fullest why I am born, what I did on this earth for you, and why I had to die. Words will come later, when I believe you need them.

"For now, go in whatever peace you can find for today, and make your life count."

Your loving Father, who really loves you and wants the best for you always. Father God, Lord Jesus, and rely on My Holy Spirit

Once more, we returned to the classroom in the "School of Hard Knocks" to learn another lesson from our instructor, the Lord. We couldn't believe this was happening to us. We had forgotten so much of what we had learned. Getting back on a right standing with God suddenly became very critical. It was very obvious that we had not balanced our lives according to God's demands. We were reminded of the time we spent (spiritually) in the belly of the fish. We tried to run then, but there was no place to hide. Here we were, repeating the same offense. Throughout our journey, God told us that He disciplines those He loves. It was up to us to turn our lives around without rocking the boat spiritually.

We were drifting in a boat without sails or covering from the Lord. We learned that our sails would have to be forgiveness and repentance, before we could get back on track again. One more time, we had critical choices to make before we could move forward.

Later that day God spoke to us again.
December 16 – **"My children, these are My words"**

"I am proud of all three of you for accepting My words the way you did. You were thinking of Me, and not yourselves.

"I know you think I am far away, but if you sink, My children, not due to your fault, I will stand in the way to help. I am still distant from you, but I live in your hearts and yes, I know where your praises remain. They are on hold with My angels, who can hear them. I will receive them when the time is right.

"Be smart! Be careful! There will be days of hot sun, cold chills, wet days, storms, and calmness. Be ready for all. Be alert and ready to watch on all sides. It is not as easy as you think. Be prepared to make each day a separate day. No two days will be alike. Watch for signs and listen for sounds.

"Stay together. You will drift only if you forget why you are in the boat. Be careful not to go over a water cliff. You will not survive. Stay where you are." God.

We were told that as we heard words, scriptures, visions, it must be confirmed by at least two people, or all three of us. If only one person heard, and the other two did not...it was not of the Lord. We were to be one unit in the boat, not three separate people drifting in one boat. He wanted us to understand that a cord of three strands is not quickly torn apart.

The situation for us was "all or none." If one person "bailed out of the boat," all three of us would sink, and the journey would end for all of us. The anxiety attacks began to surface. Without God's covering, we were so vulnerable.

During those days in the boat, each of us was separately tempted by Satan. It was a very humiliating and painful experience to be blindsided by the enemy.

We learned many valuable lessons while drifting in the boat. Among those was the sensitivity to know the difference between the voice of God and that of the prince of darkness. Three times, we were tempted to "bail out of the boat." In spite of our undeniable weaknesses, and by God's grace and unconditional love for us, we stayed together as one unit, and survived the ordeal.

December 17–**"My children, these are My words"**
"Children: As you remain in the boat, you are not alone. You have each other. You are in the boat to grow, learn and love Me more than anyone, or anything, in this world. Don't be so concerned about your days without My covering. After tonight, I will go away for a while. You are ready! Remember what you have learned these past two days. Do not forget! Your time is now starting. Be careful, be wise, and be true to Me above all else.

"The hard and difficult times are before you. Don't forget My words. When you don't know what to do, pray. Don't go by feelings. I will be back. Don't ask questions, just learn. Don't be afraid when hard times come. Read and find the answers.

"You will survive if you stay together. Be as one, and of sound mind. I will come back for you only when you are ready. Remember! Remember! Remember! You are Mine. Stay that way!

"Don't question how many days you will be in the boat. For each day you question, another day will be added. This will be another time of learning. Have patience with each other.

"Do what you know is true and right. I will come back to receive you into My arms. Be careful!

"You are still on my Pathway of Holiness and the waters could come down from all sides and crush you, just as the waters devoured the Egyptian soldiers in days of old. Sit still and don't jump. You are in the parted seas, in a sea. For now, be careful.

"Remember that I will always love you. Don't change that. Try to stay calm. Look up at times. I am there, but not where you can see or touch Me. I will return and it will be better than ever before. Go in My love.

"The days and nights may seem very dark and lonely at times. I am around, just not close.

"Learn from mistakes. This will be the last and hardest task. Go in My Name. My Holy Spirit will never leave you. Depend on Him. Walk and get direction from Him. He will show you.

"At the end, I want you to walk on the water with Me, never doubting, as you do now. I am not completely gone from you, even though it feels like it now. The stars will cover you in the night. The moon will guide your steps. During the daytime, My Holy Spirit is strong. Love on each other.

"You question how I could leave you, and why you do not receive My covering. It is because you haven't been solely dependent upon Me. Your flesh has grown deep, and is not shedding. Shed it! Get ready! I need you to be strong, but totally dependent on My breath, not yours.

"I will leave for now, but I will come back. I told this to my disciples many times and they didn't understand. You don't either. Now learn and seek. When I return you will experience things like never before. If you want it, go for it!

"Children, do not weep. Be happy this is happening. It is not good right now, and for days to come, but it will be in the end.

"I am sorry to leave, but I must go. Be strong, be wise, be godly, and go forward.

"Be careful! This boat is small and the water will be turbulent at times.

"My love goes with you always."
Your Father who loves you on earth as it is in heaven

As we drifted aimlessly in the desolate, isolated sea of confusion, from December 17 to January 12, our frustrated human emotions were constantly at the front of our minds each day. As we looked back through our journals to see what we had written, it was interesting to learn how differently each of us had reacted to the devastating and traumatic experience. There are not enough words to explain how we felt, however, we will attempt to put some of the feelings on paper.

One of us responded by relating it as a terrifying experience:

"God took his covering off of us today. How did we let this happen? Because of our total disobedience in not listening to Him the first time, the Lord placed us in a (spiritual) boat, which was only large enough to hold the three of us. We had the Holy Spirit's guidance, and He sent angels to guard us, but God did not answer our prayers for one month.

In our minds, we remembered how the Lord had often blessed us with visions, words and scriptures. Sitting in the boat, there was a strong, nervous sense that we may not ever experience those blessings again. The three of us were plagued with physical sickness, lonely days and nights, being separated from God, and terrified to move. The enemy continually tormented our spirits the entire thirty days that we drifted in the boat. Fear and anxiety consumed our lives.

For the very first time during our entire journey, we learned the fear of the Lord (fear meaning reverence), while sitting in that boat. Prior to this time in the boat, our fear of the Lord involved what He would do to us if we were disobedient. With nowhere to go, or hide, we had sufficient time to grasp the concept that it was about humbling ourselves before the Lord in reverence. He demands that there will be no other gods before Him. It saddens the Lord when He is placed second in our lives, because of our selfish actions. We comprehended that because of our lack of humility, we were now suffering the consequences. We found out that the Lord does just what He says He will do! We knew if one of us became physically sick, He would not react favorably to our cries for help. With this small thread of security shredded, it was almost more than I could handle emotionally.

The Lord said He was angry with, and disappointed in, all three of us. More than once, we heard that we had not listened and were not obedient when He told us to do something. There had been many choices and opportunities to act in obedience, but we failed to trust that all would be all right if we followed through with His instructions.

During those days in the boat, we had a variety of weather patterns, including hot, sunny, windy, dry days. Also, we experienced wet, chilly, cloudy, cold, empty days. No two days were the same, and we could not anticipate what we would have to endure with each new dawn. There we sat, in that boat, vulnerable to the elements. As we watched the weather patterns roll in, there was not one thing we could do about it, but tolerate each phase. Our words were cries of remorse, knowing we would be suffering more of the same weather. We were hoping we would not be thrown out of the boat, due to fierce weather.

All three of us were nervous and afraid when God didn't answer our prayers. He heard all of our cries and prayers, but did not answer us. He wanted us to know that we cannot do anything without His help. He also wanted us to know how it felt to be without His covering, blessings, or guidance.

We prayed prayers of forgiveness and repentance for a solid month. The Lord told us that He heard our prayers, and would have the Holy Spirit store them with the angels, until He was ready to answer them. The Lord advised us that each day we asked when we could get out of the boat, He would add one more day. This was absolutely a terrifying thought to me. I didn't know if His discipline was going to last a day, a week, a month, a year, or many years. I had anxiety attacks about staying in that boat, without covering, for a time that was beyond measure to me. There was a strong sense of vulnerability and insecurity that I had never felt since the journey began several months ago.

Knowing that we dared not ask for this to end, we were aware that we were in a place that held us captive to despair, vulnerability, loneliness, emptiness, and fear. *WE WERE ON OUR OWN. What a frightening thought.*

While in the boat, with no covering from the Lord, He was still teaching us. Even though we were there because of our disobedience, we received blessings that we were totally unaware of at the time. We had days (a month to be exact) to think about our disobedience and what we would do differently, if we could just get out of the boat. We learned about compassion, hope, faith, obedience, love, trials, and temptations. The big lesson for us was learning how to deflect Satan's attempts to steal, kill and destroy our body, mind and spirit. Each of us was tempted by the enemy during that month. We soon learned to recognize and test the spirits, when we heard the voice of the enemy. At the time, we were unaware of how powerful that lesson would be to us in the future."

The second person in the boat reacted quite differently:

"While sitting in the boat for a number of days, it became apparent to me that this was not where I wanted to be for much longer. During those days, anxiety set in as to whether it would be a short stay, or a longer period of time. I remembered being told that if we asked when we were getting out of the boat, one more day would be added to our time. It was very hard to keep my mouth shut, but having been disciplined several times on this journey, *I kept my mouth shut*. Not only was I anxious, I was angry. Not angry with God, but at myself for not being obedient and doing what we were told. That disobedience landed us in a very small boat, on a very large body of water, and I was not a happy camper (or should I say 'not a happy sailor'). Days upon days went slowly by, and I finally decided that I needed to make my amends with my Savior, in hopes of getting out of that water-borne prison. It was then that I heard, "Get out of the boat." I said, "What? Get out of the boat? Lord, is this from You? I don't want to get out of the boat and experience a spiritual drowning! Lord, You know I am slow on the uptake sometimes, but I need to be certain." I was feeling pretty good that I had just heard from the Lord, when I heard a laugh. It was the enemy playing head games with me. He was speaking to me and trying that old trick of deception, and it almost worked. I was so anxious to tell the others that we had been granted a pardon from our prison barge. However, when I told the other two, I received a slap on the hand and a rebuke. They reminded me that throughout our journey, the Lord always spoke to us, starting His instructions with the phrase, **"My children."** *Whoa*. I almost bought into the deception and I can't imagine what the consequences might have been, if we had bailed out of the boat. (Remember, the Lord said it was 'all or none'). *Oh, the enemy is so subtle. The enemy comes to steal, kill and destroy.* This was another one of our valuable lessons in the "School of Hard Knocks."

The reaction of the third person in the boat was extremely different than the first two:

"At this particular time, there was an oblivious feeling of just being relaxed and comfortable in the boat. I felt no worries, had no cares, and didn't have to wait to hear from the Lord about our next assignment. There was such contentment, as I rested in the bottom of the boat with my feet over the edge, watching the boat drift ever so slowly. The sensation was like basking in soft sand on a hot summer day, with the sun shining down. It was hard to rationalize why the other two in the boat were anxious and nervous. We were free to do what we wanted.

In the beginning, there was a slight sadness that we had gone this far in "doing things" that caused the Lord to leave us for a time. As time passed, questions began to enter my mind. Weren't the three of us responsible for each other? Was I holding the other two back? Will we disappoint each other? Am I being loyal to the Lord? Why did we let things get so far out of hand that the Lord had to leave us? Why couldn't we recall the reasons why we had to throw the stones? We didn't fear God, but we feared what He would do to us if we didn't listen. We weren't humble nor broken enough.

In our earlier assignments we went to Him every step of the way, with continuous prayers and fasting. Somewhere along the way, we started taking Him for granted and neglected His words and directions. We have not humbled ourselves in the sight of the Lord. Visions, words and scriptures were given to us to learn. Did we learn? We spoke about how the Lord had to bring others to their knees to humble them, before things would get better. We never thought that could be us. *Well, how wrong we were. It was now us.*

The eye-opening moment came when one of us heard, "Get out of the boat." At that point, total paranoia settled into my spirit. The Lord told us if even one of us jumped, it would be all over for the three of us. There would be no turning back. The journey would be over. He would choose someone else to complete the assignment that we had been given to complete. At the sound of those words, I had a vision of one of us standing at the edge of the boat, ready to jump. *"Oh, No. Don't Jump."*

For the first time in a long while, I awakened from my selfish resting and prayed, "Lord help us." In my spirit, I heard, **"It is not of Me! It is the enemy trying to get to you!"** Shouting loudly, I commanded the enemy to go away.

It was then I felt pain and was afraid in my heart. It had been half full of love for the Lord. This was not a time of celebration. The three of us had not been as "one" either. I thought if the Lord stood in front of me, would I fall on my face in reverence? Have I learned anything He has been teaching us? I know the Lord is watching over us, but at a distance. The stern words of the Lord dredged up within me, remembering that we were told He was disappointed and angry with us. However, through all of this, He still loves us. He will be waiting for us to come back to Him. He wants our lives to count. Thanking the Lord, we began to pray and humbly return to Him. All things must be to His satisfaction, not ours. The three of us prayed, asking for forgiveness, and cried in our souls for what we had done. We knew then, the Lord heard our prayers.

It was time to get out of the boat and go forward. There was a sense of excitement that we had come back to the Lord His way. Anticipation surged within us, as we waited to hear from the Lord. He is an awesome God who loves us. From the past there becomes a future."

> *The thief's purpose is to steal and kill and destroy. My purpose is to give them a rich and satisfying life. John 10:10 (NLT)*

The days of isolation in the boat drifted into weeks. We began to have more disquieted, remorseful conversations about our separation, loneliness, and wilderness wandering. Many thoughts menaced our minds and spirits. As we explained earlier, it is hard to put all of our thoughts on paper. However, these are several of the thoughts and conversations that we experienced, as we sat together in the boat:

We were so dry, and had not felt his breath on us for days. There was no peace. We did not feel life around us.

If we trusted in ourselves, we wouldn't make it. We knew we couldn't move forward if we were not clean. We had to try harder to be good and faithful witnesses to others.

Did we always try to control the situations, and was that important enough to place us in this boat?

It was critical to remember who God is, what He did, and what He will do later. Did we want to stand before God with medals or scars?

Realizing that life without love is not worth anything, we had to learn to love with our hearts and not our heads.

There were many things we would know to watch for in the future. Among them were, but not all inclusive: broken hearts for family and friends, pride, control, bullying, rejection, clarity, fear, negative authority, doubt, weariness, and lack of submission.

Lessons and thoughts continued to fill our heads throughout the idle, lifeless, thirty days in the boat. Living with anxieties had caused us to have scales on our spiritual eyes, and blindness to the truth. There had been a sense of mistrust, betrayal, and personal agendas. We had to learn to be stronger, bolder and more assertive when speaking to others.

God tells us what He will do and what He won't do. He does not ask our permission.

We were in the boat to be put back in our place. Running ahead of God, and straying from His voice seemed to be the normal course of our days. We were distracted by worldly situations, which kept us from focusing on our mission. For every turbulent day we experienced in the boat, there was a strong possibility that there would be more of the same in the coming days. An urgency to hear from the Lord consumed each of us.

> *The Lord directs our steps, so why try to understand everything along the way.*
> *Proverbs 20:24 (NLT)*

The book of Jeremiah reminded us of the compassion we felt for him, as he agonized over the message he had to deliver to the people – "Repent and turn to God." He spoke of the consequences of sin and the hope God offered. We identified with the disappointment that he felt when the people didn't listen. God was speaking to us in much the same way as Jeremiah spoke. We, too, had not been faithful in listening. However, that was about to change. Our spiritual ears and eyes were beginning to open to the voice of God. He began to speak, and we recognized it as the Lord's voice returning to us once again.

January 12–**"My children, these are My words"**

"Children, these are the words I want you to write to My children. You have sat in this boat long enough. I do not want you to become so comfortable that you don't want to get out. You learned about faith, obedience and love. It is now time to get out of the boat to fully be able to use them. Staying in the boat won't allow you to use what you have learned.

"You have learned what it is like to not hear My voice for directions.

"You have learned what it feels like to be alone, without any covering.

"You have learned what it feels like to not have My protection.

"You have learned what it feels like to be alone.

"These are the things that you will be able to share with others. You can tell others what it is like when God is not with them, or when one chooses not to have God on their side. Let them know how frightened you were, and that you wondered if you would ever be rescued. They must know that the enemy came into your boat and deceived all three of you. You have learned much more than you realize. It will be helpful for later.

"In three more days, you will all come out of the boat. It is time.

"You will be able to walk toward Me because of the love you have learned. You love Me with a special kind of love, and will come out to reach for My hand because of that love.

"You will be able to walk toward Me because of the obedience you have learned. You know you will be able to get out of the boat when I ask, because you have learned to obey My voice, and you will not be afraid.

"You will be able to walk toward Me and hold My hand, because of the strong faith you have learned. You have learned that with faith all things are possible. You will be able to do as I ask, because of your faith in Me, and not in yourself.

"When you go forward from now on, it will be the four of us walking hand in hand. I will not leave your side. We will walk, talk, love, pray, and learn of My life in a different way. For now, I want the three of you to rejoice and bask in My love, with obedience and faith. I will shield and guide you. Be aware of what is around you, and what sounds you hear. This will be a time of plenty and you will not have to be afraid. You won't doubt Me, because you have learned how much I love you. You have learned obedience and if you obey, all will be right. You have learned by faith, that all things are possible.

"Know that it is not all going to be easy. You will learn to have discernment, knowledge of right and wrong, and will detect good from evil. Through all of these assignments, you have learned not to eat from the wrong tree.

"I thank you, children, for being obedient throughout this long journey. It is not over yet. As you have learned, others need Me also. I want others to learn what you have learned, and go where you have gone. Thank you, children! I will always be here for you. We will always walk hand in hand, and I will still teach you things, but in a different way.

"For the next three days, read and prepare your hearts. Relax and enjoy this time. Lift up your praises to Me.

"I JUST WANTED YOU TO REALIZE THAT YOU CAN'T MAKE IT ON YOUR OWN!"

Your Heavenly Father, who loves you and has heard every word, every prayer, and every concern you have had while in the boat

Taking one day at a time, we realized how weak we had been in completing certain tasks on time, with little regard for a thankful heart. Having a thankful heart is a fragrant incense to the Lord. We had more than ample time to sit and think about the ways we had disrespected His authority. On many occasions, we had not blessed Him with our faithfulness, obedience and love, along the journey. The Lord reminded us that we had often placed Him as second choice in our daily schedules. He is a jealous God, and He will not allow idle chatter or earthly idols to be the god of choice. The First Commandment plainly states:

> *"You shall have no other gods before me."*
> *Exodus 20:3 (NIV)*

> *Therefore, tell the people, this is what the Lord Almighty says, "Return to me," declares the Lord Almighty, "and I will return to you," Says the Lord Almighty. Zechariah 1:3 (NIV)*

For the next three days, the Lord blessed us with uninterrupted time to pray and reflect on our entire journey. We certainly needed those three days to quiet our spirits from the traumatic experience that we had encountered in the boat. It also gave us a window of opportunity to praise Him for continuing to shower us with His mercy and grace, in spite of the rebellious actions we had displayed along the way.

At various times during our journey, the three of us had difficulty with the same three words... love, obedience, and faith. Sitting in an isolated boat, with no answers or guidance, we had many "attitude adjustments" about those very words. It was time to make positive changes, once and for all.

Even though the thirty days in the boat were painful and not what we expected, it was necessary for God to place us there. He wanted us to learn about love, obedience and faith. When we were released to get out of the boat, we felt that we had graduated to another level in the "School of Hard Knocks." There was a new excitement and enthusiasm in our spirits that we had not felt in a long time, and would be taking with us. Each of the three words with which we had struggled took on new meaning for us. We humbly share these with you at this time:

LOVE: We will be able to walk toward the Lord because of the LOVE we have learned. We will love our neighbors, because we love ourselves. Love will have a different meaning when we speak to others. We come to the Lord because we know He loves us for who we are. He has made us the way we are – in His image.

OBEDIENCE: We will be able to walk toward the Lord because of the OBEDIENCE we have learned. We were able to get out of the boat because we learned to obey His voice, and we were no longer afraid. To obey is to obey Him in all that we do. We learned that when we obey Him and do the things He tells us, the first time, we will reap a harvest of plenty. We will obey God for who He is, not who we would like to be. Thank You for making us in Your image, Lord.

FAITH: We will be able to walk toward the Lord because of the strong FAITH we have learned. We have learned with faith, all things are possible. We will be able to do as He asked because of faith in Him, not in ourselves. The faith God has instilled in each of us will be stronger, because we are now faithfully and humbly dependent on Him.

The Lord wants us to be able to see and feel the peace and wonderful things that He has prepared for, and offers to, each of us in His Promised Land. We will learn what this land has for others, and we will be able to help give them the desire, hunger and thirst to understand that journey, and experience all of His divine blessings for themselves. He desires that we all feel the love, see the richness and walk in the land of plenty, His land of milk and honey. We will hear wonderful sounds, and see all of God's creations and creatures. Oh, the glorious experience we will encounter will only be left to our imagination, until we finally reach that Promised Land.

When we go forward from now on, it will be the four of us walking together. We have the promise that God will never leave our side. We will walk, talk, love and learn of His life in a different and more responsible way. There was such a gratefulness in our hearts that we could start over and shower others with our love, obedience and faith.

The purpose of being in the boat was to bring to light that there are intense, adverse consequences when we turn away and ignore Him and try to live our lives without Him. There are also exciting results and blessings for us, if we earnestly follow directions. He always hears our cries and prayers, but sometimes it is not the right time for Him to answer us. God's timing is always perfect.

The ultimate blessing we received was the fact that our disobedience never stopped God from faithfully picking us up, dusting us off, holding us in His precious healing arms. He consistently loved on us, and showed us the straight and narrow path again. He never tired of forgiving us and loving us back into spiritual health and well being. God was and always will stay constant. Not once did He change His love for us, no matter how far from His voice we strayed.

WHAT AN UNCONDITIONAL LOVING GOD WE SERVE

ASSIGNMENT 12

GOD'S TIMELINE

PEACE

Then the angel showed me the river of the water of life, as clear as crystal, flowing from the throne of God and of the Lamb down the middle of the great street of the city. On each side of the river stood the tree of life, bearing twelve crops of fruit, yielding its fruit every month. And the leaves of the tree are for the healing of the nations... There will be no more night. They will not need the light of a lamp or the light of the sun, for the Lord God will give them light. And they will reign for ever and ever. Revelation 22:1,2,5 (NIV)

GOD'S TIMELINE

Then those who feared the Lord spoke to one another, and the Lord listened and heard them; So a book of remembrance was written before Him for those who fear the Lord and who meditate on His name. Malachi 3:16 (NKJV)

Each individual has his/her own personal journey, even though some may not recognize it as such. When we began our journey, we wondered if we were the only three who were experiencing a unique situation. We knew that the Lord had called us to take this journey together. There were many powerful, peaceful moments that confirmed the Lord was guiding us along the way. Also, during times of waywardness on our part, the results of our actions were very painful.

January 13 – **"My children, these are My words"**
"My dear children, it is so good to see your smiles and once again hear your laughter. This is

the last part of your journey, and I will be walking with you every step of the way.

"This part of your journey consists of getting your timeline ready the way I want it to look, not the way you thought it should look. You will then speak with My other children. I want them to take their own journey, the way the three of you have done. You will know how to speak to them when the time is right.

"For now, the timeline is about the four of us. It will be about the things I have put you through and for the reasons that you went through them. It is about the four of us journeying together. I know each of you had your own experiences and time with Me, but this is not what is to be put on paper. Each of you went through your own visions, scriptures and words so you could learn, but this is not what I want others to hear or see in this timeline.

"This is what is to be put on the timeline. I want to see the things you went through together, the reasons, outcome, and days, not dates. There are others who do not get visions or hear from Me. Therefore, do not put down pictures or words that pertain to you individually. Keep the walk where the three of you have been.

"What is important is the five stones. Tell why you threw them and where. People must know why you three had to complete what I put you through. (rebellion, sin) Do not make any of the drawings personal. It is not to be overly complicated. Do not be anxious for anything. Go back over the drawings and only put in what the three of you went through together. The stories will be easier to tell, because you went through them together.

"I am here to hold your hands, speak with you, and guide you through the rest of the journey. We will all decide together. I am a God of love and I need you to share this with others. I am a God who is asking for all of your obedience. I am a God who wants all to have faith that what is written in My book and all of the promises I tell, will happen!

"It is now up to you to help others achieve this. It will be completed, I am sure of this. Do not run ahead of Me. I will be here to pull you back and guide you.

"For the next three days, think about My land of plenty, milk and honey, beauty, and the timeline. It will be glorious, and we will all be together. Now get focused and be ready. Time is important to all of us. I am standing with you and My presence will not leave." Your loving Father

For the next three days, the Lord blessed us with the uninterrupted time to pray and reflect on our entire journey. We certainly needed those three days to quiet our spirits from the traumatic experience that we had encountered in the boat. It also gave us a window of opportunity to praise Him for continuing to shower us with His mercy and grace, in spite of the rebellious actions we had displayed along the way. We used part of that time to listen for more of the Lord's specific instructions about how to prepare the new timeline. (Our second one.)

January 15 – **"My children, these are My words"**

"My dear children, let me clear up some of your concerns, thoughts, wishes, directions and guidance. As I have told you, tonight we will all walk out of the boat together. We will all join hands. There is not one of you who is afraid, nor doesn't want to do this. You have listened to My words, and in most instances you obeyed at the first command. In the end, it was corrected and completed.

"Now these are the things, words, and guidance that I require the three of you to do. Tomorrow will be a day you show your love, praises, and thankfulness to Me. The next day you will pray and think about all the journeys we have been on together. For a few days longer, you will pray about each step you took, and if that is the one I want you to put down on the timeline. You may have different ideas than I have, but I am the one

who will decide the correct things to be placed on paper. Others will know and understand if they are the ones I have you draw and discuss. We have been in and out of trouble, up, and down. Not all troubles are for others to understand or hear about.

"You will go step by step, journey by journey, and ask for guidance about which of the journeys need to go on the timeline. I will guide you! As you go through each step, you will need to get a scripture about how it pertains to the Bible. It will be as the train is My path. The food is My words. Thunder are My words and reactions. Running is rebellion. I will give you scriptures to understand yourselves, also.

"Read about, and get the amount of days it took for each individual journey, the results, and the scriptures. Then it will be easier to illustrate the timeline.

"After the three of you are comfortable that you have chosen the ones I want you to have, discuss each segment. Afterward, one of you will draw them carefully and wisely, from My words, actions and directions. There will not be a real time frame. You will know when it is finished, and when I am satisfied. The person drawing the chart/timeline must pray for My guidance, to make sure this is the picture I want to portray.

"It is necessary that you follow instructions correctly the first time. You have learned what happens when you don't listen.

"Be careful to pray about everything and everyone. I am here for all of you. Do not get rebellious to one another, or step on the toes of each other. Don't try to be the master. Do not run ahead of Me! Don't eat from the wrong fruit, or pick from the wrong tree. I will walk with you and guide you each step you take.

"After the drawing/timeline is completed, you will pray for a short time, and I will tell you when to speak with the specified individual. Until then, have no concerns. It will work out as I have commanded.

"This is the most important and hardest journey in which you will partake, because it not only involves the three of you, but My other children as well. I have spoken to you about this before, but realize that is for their souls also. I need them to be with Me and not someplace else.

"I know that you are ready to listen and obey this time. It is not hard if you follow My commands. I am counting on you! As I have said before, I need you three to complete this time we have spent together, not only for you, but for others and Me.

God's Timeline

"As I have told you before, I am here. Stay with Me! Now read, find scriptures, and follow My words and directions. I AM here, Father God. The God of everyone and everything. Now go in peace, love, obedience, and faith."

As we prayed together, we wondered how we might communicate the sequences and events of a journey, if a person was listening to us relate our own story to them. First of all, we would want them to know how much God loves all of His children. He commands that we place Him first in our lives. The free will choices that we make are not always positive, but God loves on us, even when we turn away from His voice. Our desire for those listening would be for them to realize that faith to know and obedience to love God are essential to a personal walk with the Lord.

During our prayer time together, the Lord revealed to us that we were to create a visual chart/timeline portraying sequences and/or series of events, as they unfolded throughout our journey. The Lord wanted the timeline to portray both the highlights and painful, negative actions that we exhibited along the way. Many of our assignments encouraged our loyalty and obedience to venture out to make a difference in the world. Also, those times that we suffered painful consequences, due to lack of obedience, had to be included in the timeline.

Thinking about the timeline, we were aware that some would not respond positively, and others might ridicule us for our efforts. The words, illustrations and scriptures that were displayed on the timeline would be critical to the outcome of their reactions. We all agreed that it would be imperative to have the correct words and scriptures to address the difficult issues.

January 18 – **"My children, these are My words"**

"Children, remember what you learned in the boat. You asked about the timeline and what I want to have in it.

"Imagine sitting across from Me and I would be speaking with you about things I can do for you. I would like for you to imagine sitting across from each family with whom you will be speaking. These are the words which you will speak to them.

"LOVE–Tell them I love them where they are. I am going to meet them and be with them, to take over their lives of pain, troubles and desires. I want them to feel My love and know how much I do love them. The Lord is all about loving enemies, neighbors and themselves.

"OBEDIENCE–They will need to know that their obedience needs to be for the Lord. There is a way

to rid themselves of rebellious, sinful ways. They must understand and obey My commandments. When they are obedient, I will take them where I need them to go.

"FAITH – They are to have the faith to know all things will happen for good. There must be a faith to know that I will do what I have said I would do. Faith and obedience to know I love them, is essential to our walk together.

"Imagine sitting across from families that do know Me, but will not obey. There are those who have known Me all of these years, but they have no faith, nor do they believe in My love. Some know Me well, but think healings are for others and not for them. Still others have kept their "issues" as a crutch. What do you see Me having you say to them? Some have no patience to sit and listen to you. To some, your initial conversation could be a joke. You will need to have the correct words to speak that will touch all of these difficult issues.

"Pick the words that will resonate with others, not what you believe will sound good for you. They must know how I saw your lives change along the journey. Explain how your lives changed through prayer.

"It is critical that you remember who I am, and what I want to happen to others from this journey. Continue to pray and see what the total results are

from this journey. Do not rush! I do not want any disagreements among the three of you. Continue praying, reading, and doing My will. Lives will be changed, because I have the faith in all of you."

The Holy Spirit directed us to pray about each step of the journey that we had been on for several months. We were to think about and pray for direction for illustrating the timeline of our journey. We were told that not all of the journey needed to be discussed with others. Parts of it were only for the three of us to learn. The instructions were to read and get the amount of days it took to walk through each section of the journey. One of the three of us would be assigned to draw the illustrations, etc. The illustrator was to pray over each drawing to see if it was the one that the Lord wanted others to see. When each illustration was completed, the three of us were to pray over it before making the final decision.

Reviewing the journal entries about the timeline, the illustrator described how the process evolved:

"The first step was to draw a rough draft of the pictures for the timeline. As each picture was drawn, the Holy Spirit gave specific directions. Many times the words my spirit received were, 'erase, erase, erase, draw over, try again, not satisfactory.' When that happened, it was apparent that what had been drawn was not the look that would help others understand or learn about our journey. The Hand of God directed and controlled the illustrator's hand as the illustration was being drawn. We were then told to find scriptures that were relevant to each illustration that we used in our timeline. (At the very beginning of our long journey, the instructions were that each step of the journey must be scripturally based.) When the illustration and scripture was pleasing to the Lord, there was a supernatural peace that washed over our spirits, and we were allowed to move to the next phase of the timeline. There was a different feeling, as we began to understand and hear the voice of God in a whole new way. Our comprehension of His voice became deeper and more intense than ever before."

For five days we prayed for illustrations. It was an exhilarating time for us to share our stories and tasks with each other as we finalized our timeline. We sensed that this was the right time, and it made our journey come back to life once again. All three of us agreed that the discipline we had received on various occasions was painful at times, but was necessary for us to grow. Our faith, obedience and love for the Lord, would help to encourage those around us. Throughout the "School of Hard Knocks," we learned many life-changing lessons about ourselves that would enable us to be future authentic witnesses and servants for the Kingdom of God.

Two days later, the timeline was completed and we dedicated it to the Lord. We asked that everything we said, and the actions we took, would glorify His holy name as we spoke to others.

The next day, counting on the Lord to see us through, we proceeded to engage in our meeting with the one specific person that God had chosen for us to speak with earlier in the journey. This individual had many questions for us. Not having experienced a journey such as ours, it was difficult for the person to sort through and comprehend.

There will be times when you, as a reader, will go through your own journey and others will not identify with what you have experienced. Don't be discouraged. The Lord gives answers to those who truly desire to understand what is being said.

> *You must teach what is in accord with sound doctrine...In everything set them an example by doing what is good. In your teaching show integrity, seriousness and soundness of speech...*
> *Titus 2:1,7,8 (NIV)*

During the following ten days, we used our written journals to recount the entire journey. As we read, our spirits soared at the awesome ways that we received words, visions and scriptures from the Lord. It amazed us that the Lord never gave up on us. He had groomed and nurtured us for such a time as this.

We remembered those times that we were exhilarated, stunned, hopeful, doubting, prayerful, rebellious, confused, tempted, compassionate, sorrowful, joyful, and loving. It was hard for us to comprehend that we had experienced so many emotions throughout the entire journey. The Lord's presence always remained with us. It was exceedingly humbling to know that God loved us enough to redeem us from so many mistakes.

February 5 – **"My children, these are My words"**

"Children, do you know why you are so comfortable and peaceful? Look at your timeline. There is green all around, My living waters are flowing, and my sheep are still and comfortable. They are all together with their Shepherd. I am tending to them, as I am with you.

"All these words and this journey are precious to Me, and I need them to mean as much to you. You are to be speaking from your hearts only. It is plain and simple, and all about Me. Remember what I have told you all along.

"I AM who I AM, because I said so. I come first! Let it be Me! Speaking will not be hard when you remember it is all about Me.

"Make sure that all forgiveness is there. Remember how much I have loved you and took you under my wings. Remember how My angels have gone before you and continue to be with you.

"I do what I do, because I love you and all My children. They must know of the times they have gone through, and are going through now. It will be their story and strength that will live on.

"Going through it is not easy, but I am still there. We will go through things together. Make the best of it.

"Children, time is growing shorter. I need your help. Get My words and experiences out, to help those who are not sure of Me and where I am. Get ready, and be prepared. I will let you know when to move. Until then, I am here. You will see… And we will talk." God

Many times, the Lord helped us to understand what He wanted from us, by giving us visions and words. These would be learning tools for us to use, as we spoke to others. This particular vision was for the three of us. The following is an example of how God taught us through a vision.

VISION AND WORDS:

There was a door with a large, round, gold doorknob. Hearing a knock at the door, you believe you know that Jesus is on the other side. Going to the door, you put your hand on the doorknob, but are reluctant to open it. You want to believe, but there is a hesitancy. God is knocking. **"If you want to go further, you have to take a chance and open it. You can stay where you are, and always wonder, or take a chance and grab the doorknob to open it. You would be better off and much wiser if you do open the door. How long do you intend to stay where you are? As in the boat, I can leave you for as long as you want. Take a chance! Open it!"**

Life is made up of a series of events. It is said that the content of our life dictates that we place emphasis on "wholesome living," with consistent practice in learning to have obedience, faith and love. We must be grounded in truth, so that we won't be swayed by tragic circumstances, or the pull of negative emotions, that cause us to backslide.

Regardless of what has happened in our lives, we can rest assured that God walks beside all of us and holds our hand every day, because He continually loves us. He has promised us that He will never leave us or forsake us. *What an awesome thought to take with us each day.*

LIVE WHAT YOU LEARN

ASSIGNMENT 13

"I AM"

"I AM"
because
"I AM"

"I AM"

because

"I AM"

..."I am the first and I am the last; apart from me there is no God." Isaiah 44:6 (NIV)

"I AM"

God said to Moses, "I AM WHO I AM. This is what you are to say to the Israelites: I AM has sent me to you." God also said to Moses, "Say to the Israelites, 'The Lord, the God of your fathers – the God of Abraham, the God of Isaac and the God of Jacob–has sent me to you.' This is my name forever, the name by which I am to be remembered from generation to generation."
Exodus 3:14-15 (NIV)

Once again, the Lord placed on our hearts to pray for family and friends. For the next two-and-a-half months, we lifted up blessings and healing prayers for them. There were prayers for compassion in family units, family understanding and restoration, friend reconciliations, regard for parental guidance, and parental respect for faith in children. We asked that financial freedom would become a reality in each home, knowing that the power to prosper is controlled by God Himself. Prayers for restoration and stronger marriages, and love and respect for self were lifted up. We prayed for health concerns, including permanent release and healing of all addictions, and elimination of all diseases. The Lord brought to mind that we must pray for the tolerance of ethnic diversity, compassion, and respect for the less fortunate, and peer pressures for our young people. As we prayed, we asked for those same blessings and prayers of healing for the three of us and our families. It was our fervent prayer that each person would experience a healing touch from the Lord, and in turn, encounter a deeper relationship with the Lord.

March 4 – **"My children, these are My words"**

"My children, please hear My message. The journey you were on was for you, and it is also your witnesses to others about your stories and journeys. Many are on one, but don't realize it. You have taken this journey to show others you care, understand, and will be a witness to what is going on with them.

"Continue with words and scriptures for My people. When the time is right, you will go and deliver them to those I have chosen. Do not think you chose these people for such a time as this. They need My help and don't know where, or who to ask, to receive it. You are the three to go, as My witnesses, to declare My works and words.

"I will tell you when it is the right time to go. For now, continue to pray for families, just as I asked. Use time to celebrate Me also. This will end up to be the most fulfilled that you have ever felt. I orchestrated your steps and your plans. You will follow in My footsteps – in my path.

"This will be a time of complete healing for all three of you. It has already started. Now, pray and get scriptures, and anything else I have for you. Keep them written down. At the right time I will tell you and show you what you will do next. Do not worry or fret.

"Remember, don't go against Me. I am your pastor, priest, judge and jury. I have the first and the last say. Don't let Me down! I know you won't! This will be the most enjoyable, fulfilling part of the journey. Always go in peace...My peace.

"Remember, you can ask Me for anything. I decide the outcome. I do love you three and I am happy with your decisions. I will not let you down!

"Now today, go in peace and remember My love for you. I will never leave you or forsake you."
Your Loving Father, God

Throughout this journey, we were blessed to receive words, visions and scriptures from the Holy Spirit that served to guide our steps along the way. God's Word asks us to test the spirits to know if you are truly hearing from the Holy Spirit. When praying individually, there was validation that two of us, and many times all three of us, would receive the same scripture, words and/or vision.

> *Dear friends, do not believe everyone who claims to speak by the Spirit. You must test them to see if the spirit they have comes from God. For there are many false prophets in the world. This is how we know if they have the Spirit of God: If a person claiming to be a prophet acknowledges that Jesus Christ came in a real body, that person has the Spirit of God...1 John 4:1-2 (NLT)*

The following are some of the visions and interpretations that were recorded in our journals.

VISION: A glass quart jar that was filled two-thirds full of pennies.

INTERPRETATION: There was a strong sense that we were two-thirds of the way through with the "little things" (pennies represented the negative "stuff" in our lives.) When the jar became completely full, there would be no more room for the little things to control our lives, and we would live a life of freedom from bondage.

VISION: The hands of God holding a white dove. He blew the breath of life into the dove and lifted the dove upward toward heaven. The dove flew free as it was released.

INTERPRETATION: God holds us in the palm of His hand. He blows the breath of life into us, and the Holy Spirit knows the exact time that we are ready to "fly." At that time, when He feels we are strong enough, He will give us the courage and strength to move forward in freedom.

> *After his baptism, as Jesus came up out of the water, the heavens were opened and he saw the*

> *Spirit of God descending like a dove and settling on him. And a voice from heaven said,* **"This is my dearly loved Son, who brings me great joy."** *Matthew 3:16 (NLT)*

March 14–**"My children, these are My words"**

"Children, once again, you are still on another journey. I know this one is difficult, but it is for your own sake. You have prayed for, had visions and scriptures for others. You have learned to listen to My voice, with hard, disobedient choices. You have received visions and there were times they were not shown or revealed. Scriptures came and went. You have been up on the mountains, down in the valleys, set on fire, and watered down. But now this is your time. Even though you are blessings to others, you need My blessing also. Your life has been upside down for a year, trying to figure out what I want and what you think you need. You have heard My instructions and at times, you questioned, and were timid. However, at the end of each task, you always came back to Me. Now, I am here for you. Even though you have been praying blessings for My people, you are on a separate journey of restoration with your own minds, body and spirit. I know your pains. I see your tears, and I can feel your anxiousness.

"I know your hearts. They will heal and you will feel new life. The mending together is with

My strength and threads of new life. I will heal you in ways you will never realize. It will happen and you will know and feel it. I will protect you from words from others. They will be out of your hearing and reach. Remember who I am, and what I will accomplish. If you cry, it must be for Me, not others. Do not worry about others. I will take care of them.

"Listen to Me daily. You have finally started to calm your spirits. I know where your hearts have been, and the blows you have taken. I know the chances you have had to take. I will guard you and not let you fall. When you are silent, you will hear Me loud and clear. When you are still, I am working. When you read My scriptures for guidance, I have your road mapped out for you already. You will need blessings of peace. As I am one with the three of you, you are one with each other. Let no man separate the three of you. Stand strong. Stay together in one mind... The mind of Christ, My Son. We will bring you through.

"All three of you are mending for one reason or another. You have felt alone and abandoned at times. It is all right. I am here!

"Children, get back to Me. You have let other distractions take over. You are not putting your entire heart into your prayers for people. Yes, you pray, have visions and scriptures, but "What do we do?" is more on your lips. Give it up! I am working! Give up the excuses and give it all up to Me. Move over! Step aside and let Me work!

"Worry about My people. I will worry and take care of you. Now, pray for people with your whole hearts. Use discernment daily for yourselves. Be patient. Listen to Me and My voice. Scriptures and visions will come for the three of you when you are more settled. Pray in the spirit. Love in your hearts. You do not need to worry or be concerned. Keep more connected to each other.

"I AM here!

"I AM love!

"I AM righteousness!

"I AM your first and last!

"I AM because I AM!

"Continue the journey with the same excitement as you have throughout this entire journey. Good or bad, it was exciting. You are not the same now. Don't let little things stir you up or let you down. Get on with the journey and help Me enlighten these children of Mine. This is not the end, so get going! Wake up and move on!" GOD

The Lord blessed us with four days to quiet our spirits in preparation for the next assignment. Each of us experienced a serene, peaceful presence of the Lord within our spirits. Remembering that the Lord told us, **"I AM because I AM,"** there was a strong sense that our spirits were beginning to heal. The prior month in the boat had taken its toll on all three of us. Recognizing that the disobedient choices we had made were not pleasing to the Lord, we continued to be in awe that He still remained faithful to us.

One of the questions we asked as we were praying was, "God, how will You heal us?" Our question was revealed with visions and scriptures.

Visions were a vital part of our journey. We all agreed that the following vision of the two baskets of figs was one example of how we had lived our lives on this journey. There had been times that we were faithful to the Lord, and on occasion our flesh was weak. During those times, we walked away in disobedience.

<u>VISION</u>: There were two baskets of figs. One was filled with good fruit, and the other basket was full of bad fruit.
<u>INTERPRETATION</u>: The good fruit represented those who were in exile for the Lord to nurture and refine. The basket of bad fruit represented those in denial.

Immediately we received a scripture to confirm the vision.

Then the Lord said to me, "What do you see, Jeremiah?" I replied, "Figs, some very good and some very bad, too rotten to eat." Then the Lord gave me this message: "This is what the Lord, the God of Israel, says: 'The good figs represent the exiles I sent from Judah to the land of the Babylonians. I will watch over and care for them, and I will bring them back here again. I will build them up and not tear them down. I will plant them and not uproot them. I will give them hearts that recognize me as the Lord. They will be my people, and I will be their God, for they will return to me wholeheartedly. "But the bad figs," the Lord said, "represent King Zedekiah of Judah, his officials, all the people left in Jerusalem, and those who live in Egypt. I will treat them like bad figs, too rotten to eat. I will make them an object of horror and a symbol of evil to every nation on earth" ...
Jeremiah 24:3-8 (NIV)

<u>VISION</u>: We were shown a snowy white owl.

<u>INTERPRETATION</u>: God will slowly give us wisdom.

<u>VISION</u>: The mouth of God was blowing words into our spirits.

<u>INTERPRETATION</u>: He will give us knowledge and discernment.

"My wayward children" says the Lord, "come back to me and I will heal your wayward hearts."
Jeremiah 3:22 (NLT)

My child, don't reject the Lord's discipline, and don't be upset when he corrects you. For the Lord corrects those he loves, just as a father corrects a child in whom he delights.
Proverbs 3:11-12 (NLT)

VISION: A white chrysanthemum flower (a symbol that represented the three of us). All of a sudden, the flower exploded and all of the petals flew off of the flower and rose to the heavens.

INTERPRETATION: The three of us were raising our arms, praising God for our healing.

> *You have turned my mourning into joyful dancing. You have taken away my clothes of mourning and clothed me with joy, that I might sing praises to you and not be silent. Oh Lord my God, I will give you thanks forever! Psalm 30:11-12 (NLT)*

March 18 – "My children, these are My words"

"Children, I need you to move forward. Remove anything that is a hindrance to you and your growing. I have worked with you and used you to learn and separate yourselves from others. Now is the time to use what you have learned. Show what I have taught you, in My Name, My strength, My healings. You MUST move on. Go forward! I have not released you from My powerful words. I am to take over your lives.

"Do you doubt for one minute that I speak to you?

"Do you doubt for one second that I put you on a journey?

"Do you doubt Me?

"Do you believe in man and his ways?

"Do you walk on My path, or man's?

"Do you hear My voice?

"I Am"

"Do you believe in Me or other gods?

"Children, I am here for you as I have always been in your darkest days. There will be darker days and I want you clean and clear away from them. Lean on Me. Listen and watch Me more clearly. Your battle is won. I have won it for you. I, alone, am in charge of your lives. I WILL REIGN! Feel My presence. Don't take up false idols. Be of peace. From now on, you shall have quietness and experience peacefulness.

"Take some time to go over your journey. Take your timeline and review it again. You have put them down, and are forgetting where you have been, and how you got out of them.

"Don't worry about man's opinions of your journeys. If you act upon the journeys in your life, you will be more convincing to others. If you act as some, you have learned nothing. Show My love for the enemy as I have shown you. I have shared My life with you, now share with others.

"You are my beloved children, My Malachis. You have delivered My message to set you free. Now go on!

"Pray over your path. Pray for release of human flesh. Pray for My words and love to surround you. Things will start to get heated up. Stay out of the fire. Learn and walk in 'My' ways, as before. Don't lose sight of Me.

"I am your healer. I am your way. I am truth, strength and mercy. I will heal you. I will give you words, visions, and scriptures. I will be with you always.

"Don't worry, move on! Life is too short for some and not enough for others.

"I will conquer. I will grow. I truly love the three of you, and there is no one like Me or My love. Get back on track. You are not off track, but you are whining. STOP IT!

"Do the work I have asked you to do. Listen to Me and learn more from Me. If you continue in the past, you won't go to My future. You will be stuck where you are now. Go experience what is needed. Be careful what you speak. Be quiet, unless you can talk about Me.

"Listen to Me! Hear My voice! Take My directions. No more words...just actions! We will make it through this one, too."

Your loving Heavenly Father, God

We recognized that it was now time to move on and go forward. The Lord said that if we continued in the past, we would not go to His future. The three of us would be stuck right where we were at that time. The concerns we felt were about how others would react to our journey, and not about the direction the Lord had chosen for us. He wanted us to show love to those who reacted indifferently. The gift of this journey had been given to the three of us, and it was important to the Lord that we shared those experiences with others.

Words from the Lord stated that we must pray over our path. There had to be a release of the flesh to establish authenticity of this journey. If we acted upon the journeys of our life, we would be more convincing to others. The Lord expressed to us that He would give words, visions, and scriptures to help tell our story. We were instructed to choose our words carefully when speaking to others about the Lord. He wanted us to convey that He loves all of His children and His love is never ending.

The Lord brought to our attention that we had been negligent in reviewing our timeline. The specific illustrations on the timeline were for us to remember the many ways the Lord had blessed our day-to-day activities with Him. We were forgetting where we had been, and how the Lord guided us out of situations that we had created for ourselves. Our complacency and neglect was not pleasing to the Lord. On occasion, our prayers had been from the head and not the heart. We realized that we needed to get back on track and stop whining.

After all that we had been through, the Lord reminded us once again that He truly loved the three of us and would be with us always.

Throughout our journey, we received words, visions, and scriptures. Many of these were for our own clarification, discipline, encouragement and discernment. Three different times, the same vision was revealed, with different results. (These were visions of discipline.) We would like to share these three visions with you, the reader.

VISION #1: There were several horses in a starting gate, getting ready to run a race. The gates opened and a "brown horse" shot out of the gate, ahead of the rest of the horses.

INTERPRETATION: The Holy Spirit revealed, **"False Start! Do not get ahead of Me. Go back and wait for Me."** There was a sense that the horse was one of us, who was running ahead of God and not waiting for Him to give specific directions. On occasion, all three of us had run ahead of God. This vision was a reality check to show that God was still in charge. For three weeks the vision of the brown horse was not addressed again, because of the fear of more discipline. Finally, courage came to ask the Lord if the horse was ready to go back to the starting gate. Pride and ego encouraged the thinking, that surely, three weeks was enough time to make things right. Oh, little did we know!

VISION #2: The "brown horse" was observed standing in the stall at the Livery Stable. The horse was bridled and tethered in place, with its head peering out of the top door of the stall.

INTERPRETATION: It was very obvious that the horse was not at the starting gate. Bridled and tethered in the stall of the Livery Stable, the feeling was that the brown horse would be out of the race for a length of time because of its lack of discipline. Sensing that the brown horse could have been any one of the three of us, we knew we had much work to do within ourselves, before we would be allowed to run the real race in life. For the time being, there were many lessons to learn. With the Lord's guidance and protection, there was hope that the "brown horse" (us) would one day be released and set free. It would be several months before the Lord allowed another vision of the "brown horse" again. During those months, the "brown horse" (each of us) remained in the stable, learning about pride, humility, discipline and obedience.

After spending thirty days in a lonely, isolated boat, it was at that time, the Lord revealed, for the third time, the vision of the "brown horse."

VISION #3: The "brown horse" was racing through a green pasture with the other horses, never to be bridled again. It was kicking up its heels in freedom.

INTERPRETATION: The Lord was saying that the "brown horse" would never be bridled again. (Meaning that we would never carry the weight of those burdens again.) There was freedom to make wise choices and live a life free from the pains of the past.

For the next two weeks we continued to pray blessings into the lives of families and friends. As we prayed for others, there was a sense that the peace of the Lord was filling our spirits, also.

April 5–"My children, these are My words"
"Children, some day you will tell My story. It will have to be told. You will speak to others and show My stories to many. Our journey, love, and troubled times will be shared. All will need to know the outcome of our journey.

"Don't worry about what others say about you, because it will be those who never understand and won't listen. But, they will need to hear to help them.

"I will give you the words and directions, and what part of the journey they will need to hear, that will enable them to understand. You won't need to tell the entire story to everyone. It may be just bits and pieces. I will put the words and actions upon you.

"The second part of your journey will be starting soon. Pray, read, and go in peace. I am here and we will need to start shortly. Continue to honor Me and walk in My ways. Don't get disconnected or lose closeness with Me and each other. It will get easier. Don't worry! You will each find your place.

"I need you to write down your words and feelings about being set apart from your family, loved ones, children and friends. Write them individually, then come together to discuss what you have written. It will be used later in your next journey. This will be important to others later on. Enjoy, praise, laugh and sing. I am with you.

"Continue to write and pray. This healing is an important part of your journey. Protect it and yourselves. You will be all right and come out whole. My love as always." God

Knowing that we would soon be receiving another assignment, we wanted to spend dedicated time to acknowledge and praise the Lord for bringing us out of our time of wilderness. For nine days we consciously lifted up praises to the Lord for watching over us while we struggled through trials, temptations, and hard lessons. It made us smile to think about all of the people and circumstances that God keeps track of, yet He specifically took time to care for our spiritual needs and physical safety. He loves all of His children equally.

April 24 – **"My children, these are My words"**
"Children, you are getting ready to go to the next step. I know you are excited for completion. Continue to pray, especially for each other.

"As I have asked before, write down the words you continue to have difficulties with, then the three of you must pray over them. You will, once again, get words and/or visions. Find out what I want you to do with them, and then come together again and pray for them. Then, and not until then, will we be able to move on.

"I am with you and I will help you. There is no need for concern. Your hurts, insecurities, wrongdoings, and pain will be finished. We will move forward to the next part of your journey. Until then, be careful and pray. Feel My presence with you always." Your loving Father, God, Jesus and My Holy Spirit.

The Lord encouraged us to continue praying for families and friends. He never tires of receiving our concerns and praises. It was definitely a time of joy and excitement for the three of us to celebrate that we were no longer in a spiritual famine. We rejoiced that we had learned lifelong lessons along the way. Throughout this journey, we suffered many painful consequences as a result of our wayward behavior. However, in every circumstance, and every lesson, we thanked God for the tools we were given that may encourage others in the future.

May 5 – **"My children, these are My words"**

"My children, stay steady on the road you are traveling. I am proud of your spirits. You are learning as Abraham did. SACRIFICE AND I WILL SUBSTITUTE for you. I am still working with you.

"I am sending others to you, so stay prepared. Remember your walk, your words and your actions. You will remember more than you realize. Continue to stay focused.

"Listen carefully to words! Things will change. My words will begin to come alive and have true meanings. Continue to read and feel joy from My words. I am here, so walk with Me and we will journey on." Faithfully, God

We won't really know the depth of our character until we see how we react under pressure. Our hearts were mending and much time was spent in reflection of how we had handled all the pressures of our journey. There was such a gratefulness that the Lord held our hand and walked beside us during the times we struggled. We were beginning to see that all of those times had been opportunities of growth. It was as if a veil had lifted and we were being shown how our character and countenance had been challenged, as we traveled each path of the journey.

The three of us agreed that actions speak louder than words. Our goal for the future was to do just that. We had been given the tool of wisdom, by which trials are overcome. We can ask for God's wisdom to guide all of our choices. He will never leave us alone with our problems, because He generously supplies everything we need. Our God is an awesome God!

COUNT THE NUMBER OF RAINBOWS, NOT THE NUMBER OF THUNDERSTORMS

ASSIGNMENT 14

"TODAY AND FOREVER"

LIVING WATERS

He who was seated on the throne said, **"I am making everything new!"** *Then he said,* **"Write this down, for these words are trustworthy and true."** *He said to me:* **"It is done. I am the Alpha and the Omega, the Beginning and the End. To him who is thirsty I will give to drink without cost from the spring of the water of life. He who overcomes will inherit all this, and I will be his God and he will be my son."**
Revelation 21:5-7 (NIV)

"TODAY AND FOREVER"

This is the day the Lord has made; let us rejoice and be glad in it. Psalm 118:24 (NIV)

For the past six days, there had been a sense of peace in knowing that we had been obedient in praying for family and friends. We thanked the Lord for giving us joyful hearts to pray and complete one more of our assignments.

May 11 – **"My children, these are My words"**

"My children, to get to the next level, your next journey, there are some things I need for you to do. You will need to be silenced with obedience, and then you will get your direction. It will be another part of the journey that is going to make the three of you stronger once again.

"You must do just as I am asking. Do not put your own spin on it. Do not add to or subtract from it either. I will explain and you will just do

it. It will be a time of refreshing and regeneration to the three of you.

"At this time, we will really be getting close to one another with your facts and reconciliation. You must all be on the same page again, with the same ideas and attitudes.

"I do not want any separation of thoughts. You will need to bond differently than most everyday bonding. It is a time of My love sinking into each other's lives. You must be one in spirit, to realize who I am. Be strong in your faith for Me. As three cords, woven into one, makes the cord stronger, you three will grow stronger in your faith.

"Don't worry, it will be fine. For such a time as this, you will work together. The future is Mine to hold.

"These are the things you will do daily for thirty days. Each day you are to do as each day is laid out.

1. Today praise Me.
2. Today read to Me.
3. Today pray with Me.
4. Today walk with Me.
5. Today sing to Me.
6. Today read My scriptures.
7. Today have mercy.
8. Today love.

"Today And Forever"

9. Today listen to My voice.
10. Today have patience.
11. Today feel life.
12. Today be gentle.
13. Today show happiness.
14. Today show compassion.
15. Today help someone.
16. Today phone a loved one.
17. Today have no arguments.
18. Today give hope to someone.
19. Today have healing words with someone.
20. Today send a note of thanks.
21. Today tell someone how much you love them.
22. Today let it be a day of silence.
23. Today let it be a day of obedience.
24. Today is there happiness in your heart?
25. Today make all good decisions.
26. Today read.
27. Today speak in the spirit to Me.
28. Today let there be peace in your heart.
29. Today listen to directions.
30. Today is your day of hope and time to go on to your new journey.

"Each day as you have been doing, speak and pray with each other. Go over what you did for the day and help each other with words of

encouragement. Be patient with one another. Get together and pray. You have not done this in a long time, and it is overdue. Don't let schedules of other things get in your way of My work. Be patient, be still, and work together as one.

"My children, now you will be ready to move in the direction I have wanted you to move all along. Finish this task first. We will speak again."

Your Heavenly, Faithful Father, God

Once again, God reminded us that His ways are not our ways. Nor does His day coincide with our calendar days. He instructed us to spend thirty days (His thirty days) reflecting on, and reviewing, the following topics. According to our calendar days, we remained on this assignment for ninety-one days.

Even though the Lord said "today," it became apparent to us that it was not just one day. There were times that we prayed from one to five days on each topic.

TODAY PRAISE ME

There were praises for His faithfulness to take care of us physically, mentally, emotionally, and most of all, spiritually. It was a joy to praise Him with our offerings, singing, thanksgiving of songs and hymns, and for Jerusalem. For three days we gave thanks to His Name for whatever is true, honorable, right, pure, and lovely. There were praises to Him for health, family, friends, and animals. He loves us enough to save us from disasters and right and wrong decisions, and for just loving us. We were so grateful that the Lord was walking with us, and sending us out on assignments. There was an awareness that God was pouring blessings into us, and taking the negative things away for our own safety and peace. We praised Him for each day's miracles that we could visibly see, and for those unseen by us, but experienced by others.

TODAY READ TO ME

Two days were spent reading scriptures and prayers out loud to each other from the Psalms and Proverbs. Reading aloud enabled us to audibly worship and praise the Lord. As we read from the scriptures and listened to our own voices giving the Lord praise, honor and glory, we experienced a peace that comes from knowing that the Word of God is tried and true.

> *I will exalt you, my God and King, and praise your name forever and ever. I will praise you every day; yes, I will praise you forever. Great is the Lord! He is most worthy of praise! No one can measure his greatness. Psalm 145:1-3 (NLT)*

PRAY WITH ME

Perhaps you talk to God on a regular basis, but you don't feel like you are getting through. You get distracted with the duties of the day. You can't get yourself in a quiet mood to communicate with the Lord. Your intentions are very honorable, but the physical body is exhausted from the burdens of the day. Yet, you want results, without the effort. Does that describe a few of us? Prayer isn't just words to get what you want, nor is it based on your feelings. God doesn't judge us by how long we pray, or if we use impressive words. Sometimes prayer is a place of silence and solitude, where you can find hope and restoration. Other times you find yourself wrestling and struggling with God, trying to make amends and confessing the things that you have done, that you know are not pleasing to God. Either way, we can celebrate in thankful prayer, that God understands us and meets us where we are that day. We can stay connected to God through prayer, which allows the Holy Spirit to empower and energize us. During the next two days we prayed thanksgiving prayers for various situations, to include, but not limited to, family, finances, health, world conditions, thankfulness, praises, and relationships. After our quiet time with the Lord, we read the Gospels of Matthew and Luke from the Bible.

WALK WITH ME

A total of five days were spent walking, talking, praying and singing to the Lord. We reflected on each path that we had walked with the Lord during our entire journey. God placed us on a path of His choosing. Our path was sometimes steep and slippery, but, throughout all of it, the Lord gave us His abundant strength and peace to move forward. The Lord reminded us that the road we traveled together was ultimately a highway to heaven. When we considered this radiant destination, the roughness or smoothness of the road ahead became much less significant. It has not been a coincidence that the three of us have traveled together for such a time as this. We remembered how we walked with the Lord, and how we were disciplined when we denied the Lord. Throughout this journey, God ALWAYS loved us back into wholeness so we could continue to study and learn about His faithfulness, in spite of our shortcomings. One of our favorite songs was "In the Garden," which states that God walks with us and talks with us and tells us that we are His own. We were so grateful for His faithfulness to watch over and walk with us.

TODAY SING WITH ME

We listened to and sang our favorite praise songs for the next two days. We even sang our favorite childhood songs… "Jesus Loves Me," "In the Garden," "Jesus Loves the Little Children." We audibly sang our prayers and scriptures for those two days. At first, it was out of our comfort zone to sing the prayers that would normally be said silently. It soon became a new way for us to reach out to the Lord with thankfulness. Even though singing may not be your gift, the Lord loves to hear our voices, because our melodies are a fragrant incense/sacrifice being lifted up to His throne room of mercy and grace.

TODAY READ MY SCRIPTURES

A portion of the two days of reading scriptures, were spent reviewing Joshua 4. This was a reminder of how God had spoken to the Israelites during their journey of exile. We identified with this scripture, because we, too, were on our own journey with the Lord. There were times that we had been rebellious, the same as the Israelites. We prayed that the scriptures that had become so familiar to us, and any new scriptures, would have more fruitful meaning to them. To relate the message to others, we prayed for a new understanding of the words.

TODAY HAVE MERCY

For two days the three of us talked about the word mercy, and wondered if, deep down, we really felt it in our spirits. We discussed this and said that we didn't grasp how to pray for mercy for others, or for ourselves. Praying, we asked God to show us in a way that we would understand.

"Today And Forever"

The following was one of the visions about mercy that the Lord revealed to us.

VISION: The Lord showed us many faces. Their eyes were swollen and red from weeping. A few had big tears streaming from the corners of their eyes. There were faces of old men and women, young people, children, all with faces that reflected stress and hopelessness for their future.

INTERPRETATION: We sensed that God was telling us we will need to feel their pain, and show much compassion for those less fortunate and downtrodden. People will be in despair and have little hope, with no place to turn for comfort. We were told that we would see those faces again. There would be many, and we needed to understand the pain that they exhibited, and show them love, mercy, and compassion during their times of need.

TODAY LOVE

What would it take for us to spread love, pray for, and breathe in love, then pour it out on others? Love is just like a fire, it needs attention. If left unattended, both love and fire will ultimately burn out, leaving just a pile of ashes, instead of a warm glow. Our thoughts, words, and actions would need to be scrutinized and refined, so that others would feel the authenticity of our actions. These two days left us with much food for thought.

LISTEN TO MY VOICE

Throughout our journey, we each found a place in our home that we called our "quiet place" to meet with the Lord. One of us seemed to hear and speak with the Lord while taking a daily shower and/or sitting in a chair in the bedroom. Another often received words in bed, during the very early morning hours. Still another found peace and quiet in their special recliner. We prayed to be able to hear His voice, whenever and wherever He chose to speak. Sometimes it was hard to recognize when He was speaking, because we were distracted by daily routines and chores. Learning to tune out the distractions of the day was a decision that each of us had to make. It took extreme effort on our part, to devote time to the Lord on a daily basis. We knew that we could no longer place Him as "second best." These next two days were very peaceful and comforting for all three of us. During our quiet time, we received the following scripture:

> *"I tell you the truth, anyone who sneaks over the wall of a sheepfold, rather than going through the gate, must surely be a thief and a robber! But the one who enters through the gate is the shepherd of the sheep. The gatekeeper opens the gate for him, and the sheep recognize his voice and come to him. He calls his own sheep by name and leads them out. After he has gathered his own flock, he walks ahead of them, and they follow him because they know his voice. They won't follow a stranger, they will run from him because they don't know his voice." John 10:1-5 (NLT)*

"Today And Forever"

TODAY HAVE PATIENCE

It is often said, "Patience is not one of my virtues." The word patience means: the power or capacity to endure without complaint, something difficult or disagreeable.

The three of us were totally aware that we needed to use the next two days examining our attitudes and actions, regarding how patient we were with each other and our families. We wanted to be ready for positive action when we were called to a task or assignment. Using Job as one of our references regarding the word patience, we began to reevaluate ourselves to prepare for a lifetime of changes for the better. The Lord reminded us of our own journey. During each lesson, God was teaching us about His patience with us, and how He expected and demanded our love, patience, and obedience in responding back to Him.

We reflected on the patience of Job and his ability to endure long suffering. There were so many lessons to be learned from his journey with the Lord.

> *For examples of patience in suffering, dear brothers and sisters, look at the prophets who spoke in the name of the Lord. We give great honor to those who endure under suffering. For instance, you know about Job, a man of great endurance. You can see how the Lord was kind to him at the end, for the Lord is full of tenderness and mercy.*
> *James 5:10-11 (NLT)*

TODAY FEEL LIFE

Our desire was to feel life in the Lord. Experiencing the gift of love that the Lord was pouring into us was overwhelmingly peaceful to all three of us. Life has its ups and downs, but our prayer was to learn how to feel life in the fullest each day. Emotions help guide us through life. During any given day, we, as human beings, experience the emotions of love, happiness, disappointments, compassion, joy, guilt, anger, peace, and many others. To change the way we feel, we need to adjust our thinking. God longs to make our life a glorious adventure, but we should stop clinging to our old ways. With God's help, we can receive the fullness of His love, simply by honoring Him each day with thankful prayers. For two days, we concentrated on the awesome ways that God has chosen to love on us. Part of this lesson was to thank Him daily for our lives, and His unending, unconditional love for us.

TODAY BE GENTLE

Gentleness is displayed in many forms. God has a way of showing us many unexpected glimpses of the ways He loves on and cares for us. He sends gentle breezes that refresh us. Day after day, He lovingly paints glorious, vivid sunsets across the skies, just for our enjoyment. The phenomenal panoramic view of a rainbow exploding across the horizon in all of its spectacular beauty is another perfect example of

God's gentle promise that He will always provide for and be there for each of us.

Mary, the mother of Jesus, gently held her tiny baby in her arms after He was born in humble and uncomfortable surrounding. We, too, should try to display gentleness and compassion to the less fortunate during their uncertain times.

We remembered that we had not always been gentle and caring along our journey. In spite of those weaknesses, we gratefully dedicated prayers of thanksgiving to the Lord for providing us the tools, which included a renewed spirit of compassion and enthusiasm to be His voice of hope and peace.

> *Always be humble and gentle. Be patient with each other, making allowance for each other's faults because of your love. Make every effort to keep yourselves united in the Spirit, binding yourselves together with peace. Ephesians 4:2-3 (NLT)*

For three days, we prayed for the Lord to strengthen us from the inside out, to be more aware of our actions, words and deeds.

TODAY SHOW HAPPINESS

Happiness is of our choosing. Unless we allow it, no one can take the joy and happiness from us. God gave each of us the freewill to make good choices that affect us and others. Three days of thanking God for His mercy and grace filled our hearts to overflowing with gratitude, for the lessons He had instilled in each of us. He speaks to us continually: through sights, sounds, thoughts, impressions and scriptures. All He asked of us was to be attentive to His messages, in whatever form they came. There was an awareness that we had a new chance to make a positive difference in the lives of others, just by keeping our attitude in tune with God's expectations for us.

> *When times are good, be happy; but when times are bad, consider: God has made the one as well as the other. Therefore, a man cannot discover anything about his future. Ecclesiastes 7:14 (NIV)*

TODAY SHOW COMPASSION

Sometimes others may be in need of compassionate words to keep their spirits alive. We realized that we must daily give words of encouragement to those who were struggling for one reason or another. For three days we were reminded that our loving God had shown us such deep compassion when we were a source of disappointment to Him at times. He always loved us back into wholeness when we were at a low point on our journey. The Lord equipped us to speak encouraging words to those who needed to know that God would also love them unconditionally. Even a smile while standing in line at the grocery store can restore a sense of joy in others. A smile is the same in any language. During the holidays, many who have

"Today And Forever"

suffered losses need compassion and understanding. A loving touch or hug from us reminds them that they are not alone. Each of us can be that sunburst of the glory of God.

TODAY HELP SOMEONE

During our journey, the Lord constantly spoke to us about the importance of serving one another. He cautioned us about having the right motives in helping others. For the next two days we discussed past times when we had placed ourselves first, instead of focusing on the needs of others. We were reminded of the Bible story about the Good Samaritan who had compassion for the man lying on the side of the road and took care of him. (The entire story is found in *Luke 10:30-37.*) We came to realize that our neighbor is anyone who is in need of help. Wherever you look, there are people crying out for help. All of us can be good Samaritans and treat them as people to love.

If one falls down, his friend can help him up. But pity the man who falls and has no one to help him up! Ecclesiastes 4:10 (NIV)

Therefore, strengthen your feeble arms and weak knees, "Make level paths for your feet," so that the lame may not be disabled, but rather healed. Hebrews 12:12-13 (NIV)

TODAY PHONE A LOVED ONE

As we looked back on our journey together, we gratefully discussed how the Lord had helped us through all of our difficult times. Had we not relied upon Him to hear our prayers for strength and understanding during those times, we would not have the desire to be His hands and feet today. Many times communication with family members or friends become far down on our list of priorities. For two days, the Lord embedded thoughts in our minds that we must make a conscious effort to communicate with family members or friends. Unless there is a dialog, we may never know if they are on a long, uphill journey and their energy is almost spent. Just as the Lord had lifted our spirits when we felt downtrodden, we knew that one simple phone call with cheerful, encouraging words may have been an answer to a long-awaited prayer. Our minds went back to those times that our spirits soared, just by hearing the voice of our loved ones. We remembered the excitement of just knowing that they cared enough to make that phone call. Those two days gave us a new awareness that God is at the center of every move we make, even if it only involves making a simple phone call.

TODAY HAVE NO ARGUMENTS

When the challenges of life stare us in the face, we may need help from others to love and support each other with empathy, love and kindness. During

"Today And Forever"

this day of reflection, the Lord placed in our spirits that we should not be so self-absorbed that we forget to ask how others around us are doing. There was a strong sense that He was telling us that we should remain positive, peaceable and considerate when discussing issues with others. We should build each other up, not tear each other down. Sometimes we may not always agree, and may have different opinions; however, we should respect and seek to view them as significant, worthy and valuable. Like honey, the words from our mouth should be sweet to the soul and healing to the bones.

> *Don't have anything to do with foolish and stupid arguments, because you know they produce quarrels. And the Lord's servant must not quarrel; instead, he must be kind to everyone, able to teach, not resentful. 2 Timothy 2:23-24 (NIV)*

TODAY GIVE HOPE TO SOMEONE

Genesis 12 reveals the whole story of how Abraham, at seventy-five years of age, faced an uncertain future. He listened when God called him to pack up his family and move to a faraway region. Abraham in faith, accepted God's words of **"Go and I will show you."**(*Genesis 12:1*) Because of his obedience and hope, the world will never be the same. We all have a story, and we are right in the middle of it. We can look ahead in paralyzing fear, or move forward expectantly with hope for the future. Five days of intense dialog with each other brought a reality that we, too, could give hope to those who may be downtrodden because of circumstances beyond their control. Knowing that we could not live on yesterday's passions, we had to learn how to relate to people through God's unlimited supply of love, not our own. Prayers strengthen hope as we lean on and trust the One who knows and loves us as His own.

> *"For I know the plans I have for you," declares the Lord, "plans to prosper you and not to harm you, plans to give you hope and a future."*
> *Jeremiah 29:11 (NIV)*

TODAY HAVE HEALING WORDS WITH SOMEONE

There are times relationships need to be restored. Sometimes the healing words have to begin with us, and are those that are spoken internally. If we have a strained relationship with an individual, it should be considered a priority for us to examine our conscience and determine the motive for the division. We get tired and want to give up on trying to "fix things ourselves." Many times it is those mis-communicated words that create relational breakdowns with those we love the most. Gentle, kind, and loving gestures often speak louder than words and often help "clear the air," where healing needs to occur. Healing encompasses many aspects of our lives. There may be a need to pray with someone for a physical healing.

Others may need spiritual encouragement, while another may be crying out for emotional healing. The Lord reminded us, for these two days, that He had given us tools of healing scriptures and words to be the hands and feet of Jesus (meaning to speak, act and walk as Jesus.) Our perseverance and prayers may be the actions and words that others need to fully experience their healing.

TODAY SEND A NOTE OF THANKS

The Lord reminded us that sending a note of thanks is not always a printed word. Often times it is written on our heart for God to read. God is truly blessed by our internal love notes of thanksgiving. It awakens our awareness to a multitude of blessings. The effort of finding the right words to say or write often discourages many of us from doing anything. There was a consensus that we needed to make some changes in the way we showed thankfulness. It is impossible to know whose life we may touch. Their journeys are different than ours. A simple note of thanks may be the lifeline of hope and gentle encouragement that is needed for another person. They may have read that note over and over daily, which gave them courage to explore a deeper relationship with the Lord. We acknowledged that we, too, are sometimes weak. A kind and gentle word from others is affirmation to us that others care. Love notes can be received from God on a daily basis. Why not pass that blessing forward?

TODAY TELL SOMEONE HOW MUCH YOU LOVE THEM

Each of us has a need to be loved. It should be a spontaneous response to tell others that we love them.

Love is much more than just warm, fuzzy feelings. It is an attitude that we reveal to others by our actions. For the next two days, we were prompted to show love by helping when it wasn't convenient, and by giving when we, ourselves, were exhausted. The Lord wanted us to devote energy to the welfare of others instead of our own. The reaction from others was an amazing experience. Their facial expressions and demeanor softened, as they received our heartfelt love and attention. It was a good reminder to us that love doesn't always have to be spoken aloud. Actions of love speak volumes sometimes. We also grasped the concept that speaking words of love to others may be the one encounter that resulted in peaceful healing to their body and their soul. Jesus commanded us to love one another:

> *So now I am giving you a new commandment. Love each other. Just as I have loved you, you should love each other. Your love for one another will prove to the world that you are my disciples."*
> *John 13:34-35 (NLT)*

TODAY LET IT BE A DAY OF SILENCE

> *"Be still and know that I am God! I will be honored by every nation. I will be honored throughout the world."* Psalm 46:10 (NLT)

Many times throughout our journey, the Lord placed a heavy hand on us, because we did not take the time to sit in silence and listen for His voice when He was giving us instructions. More than once, we found ourselves saying, "Were those just my human thoughts, or did that voice come from the Lord?" Thinking back on those specific times, we realized that we were trying to make our own way on the journey, instead of following the path that the Lord had already prepared for us. Had we just sat in silence and listened for the Lord to speak to us, we would have eliminated the need for the Lord's heavy hand of discipline. Spending two days in silence encouraged all three of us to reevaluate how we spent our time, and also the amount of time we dedicated to the Lord each day. It became very evident that we had failed in many areas and we needed to be more disciplined in our time management with the Lord. We challenge you to do the same. His words of wisdom are invaluable to show each of us how to have a deeper, fulfilling relationship and walk with Him in the future.

TODAY LET IT BE A DAY OF OBEDIENCE

Deuteronomy 8:1 tells us to obey God's commandments. During the three days of reflection concerning obedience to Him, we were reminded, again, that there are several ways we can do this. We can remember to obey God with our heart, will, mind, body, and finances. The heart allows us to love Him more than any relationship, activity, achievement or possession. Our will enables us to be strong enough to commit ourselves completely to Him. Our mind determines how we seek to know Him and His word, so that it forms a foundation of all we think and do. Our body and all of our strengths, talents and sexuality are given to us by God to be used according to His rules, not ours. Ultimately, all that we have comes from God. We are not the owners of our finances, only managers and overseers of them. Sometimes there is negligence to be good stewards of all that has been given to us. Discussions and prayers concerning obedience prompted us to be more grateful that God has given each of us many chances to change our attitudes and behaviors. God demands our obedience in all that we do and say. He also instructs us to practice what He teaches us.

> *"Be careful to obey all the commands I am giving you today. Then you will live and multiply, and you will enter and occupy the land the Lord swore to give your ancestors."...* So obey the commands

"Today And Forever"

> *of the Lord your God by walking in his ways and fearing him. Deuteronomy 8:1, 6 (NLT)*

TODAY IS THERE HAPPINESS IN YOUR HEART?

How do we define happiness? Is it the news that you and your spouse are soon to be parents? Perhaps happiness is receiving the word that you just got that promotion and a substantial increase in salary. It may be having the grandchildren visit for a sleep over on the weekend. Our animals give us unconditional love and add joy to our lives. Music is another way of experiencing happiness. The Lord says that laughter is the best medicine. There are countless reasons to have happiness in your heart. However, the most awesome and rewarding is to know that the Lord loves you and desires to bring you the joy and peace that can come from Him living in your heart. It was easy for the three of us to spend four days reflecting on the ways that God has given us the joys of our life. As we went through the "School of Hard Knocks," the Lord often reminded us that our obedience to surrender our hearts to the Lord also blessed Him. We will find true happiness if we put our relationship with God above all earthly riches. Happiness is a way of travel, not a destination.

> *A happy heart makes the face cheerful, but heartache crushes the spirit. Proverbs 15:13 (NIV)*

TODAY MAKE ALL GOOD DECISIONS

We knew that we had not fully surrendered our decision making to the Lord in the past. For the next four days, we made a conscious effort to be aware of each and every decision we made. A good decision is one that is prayed over, blessed, and knowing in your heart that it is correct. Throughout our journey, we learned from the Lord that if you do not know what to do, don't do anything until you feel a peace that the decision is correct. One of the incredible gifts that each of us has received is the assurance that God will still love and protect us, even if we get off track for a period of time.

TODAY READ

Throughout our journey, the three of us were told that we needed to spend more time reading the scriptures. We were reminded that distractions from the busy routines of the day took our focus to a place that was not pleasing to the Lord. It was so comforting to know that the Lord kept His hand on us, in spite of our shortcomings. For four days we confessed our weaknesses and asked for renewed energy and discipline to make the changes in our lives that were needed. We were encouraged to get into the Word on a daily basis. Each of us went to our own personal quiet space in our home to read and commune with the Lord. Four days of making a conscious effort to be disciplined in reading God's Word helped us to regain structure in our lives. Once again, our hearts began to stir and to hunger in an intense way. The desire was to seek the Lord and learn more of His ways. God wants all of us to be totally prepared for His return. None of us know when that day will be, but we do know there will be no second chances when that day occurs.

> *Blessed is the one who reads the words of this prophecy, and blessed are those who hear it and take to heart what is written in it, because the time is near. Revelation 1:3 (NIV)*

TODAY SPEAK IN THE SPIRIT TO ME

God, in His infinite wisdom, gives hope to His children. As descendants of the Most High God, we are not left to our own resources to carry our burdens. Even when we don't know the right words to pray, the Holy Spirit prays for and with us. We don't need to be afraid to come before the Lord. The Holy Spirit is in direct harmony with God's will. We can trust that the Holy Spirit will intercede in our behalf. Then, when we bring our requests before the Lord, He will always do what is best. God works in "everything." During the four days of praying, we admitted our weakness in recalling the numerous times that we were at loss for words to pray as we struggled for answers. Sometimes, it was not only loss of words, we didn't even know the right thing for which to hope. He didn't promise that the path would be easy, but He did promise to protect us and walk that path with each of us. The Holy Spirit is our constant companion, in you, with you, and upon you. It just doesn't get any better than that, dear friends.

> *In the same way, the Spirit helps us in our weakness. We do not know what we ought to pray for, but the Spirit himself intercedes for us with groans that words cannot express. And he who searches our hearts knows the mind of the Spirit, because the Spirit intercedes for the saints in accordance with God's will. Romans 8:26-27 (NIV)*

TODAY LET THERE BE PEACE IN YOUR HEART

For most of us, life is busy. The peace we find is often short-lived. We have so much to think about during any given day. There are the kids, our jobs, the house payment, our health, among many other things. We mean well. We want prayer to be our priority, but we are too busy chasing our toddlers all day. Or, we have to get up at 5:00 a.m. for that long commute to work, and the list goes on. Then, we wonder why peace is so elusive. We forget to call on the One who replenishes our source of peace and calms our storms. However, in the midst of turmoil we can learn new habits. It is rare that peace comes naturally. It has to be learned. Too often our hearts are not still or silent and we are not able to hear God's voice speaking to us. Making time for ourselves is vital to our inner spiritual growth. Invite God to give you a hunger for His Word. We can have powerful prayer lives when we are fed spiritually. In turn, we can pour out on others those blessings of peace and hope that have become our normal way of life.

For six days we prayed for peace. One of us received the words "PREPARE, PREPARE." We asked the Holy Spirit to reveal to us the reason we were to prepare.

This vision that the Lord revealed to us represents peace and encouragement.

VISION: A hand/arm (hand of God) reaching down to earth from heaven. INTERPRETATION: The world as we know it is changing. In the midst of the turmoil, we are to reach out and hold on to the promises of God. His Word says that He will never leave us or forsake us. We must be prepared each day by studying His Word, trusting His promises, and living a life that is pleasing to the Lord. All of these things will bring us peace and in turn, we can encourage others to have a deeper relationship with the Lord. His hand is always available to us if we will only look up, reach for, and cling to the loving, peaceful, faithful, security that only God can give to each of us.

TODAY LISTEN TO DIRECTIONS

Throughout our lives, people have been giving us directions. Our parents gave us directions to "do this, or don't do that." Teachers gave us directions in acquiring knowledge. Traffic signals give us directions to stop or go with the light. The fact is, we have been receiving directions from various sources and people all of our lives. But the most important directions needed are those given to us by the Lord our Savior. He gives us wisdom and knowledge to live an honest, moral and spiritual life that is pleasing to Him. Have we always followed directions from our parents or teachers? *Absolutely not.* Have we always followed directions from the Lord? *Absolutely not.* We have all fallen short and are guilty of following our own path. It was obvious that we had been given many specific directions along the journey, and had disregarded many of the instructions given to us. Prayers asking for forgiveness and repentance formed on our lips several times during the four days we revisited our journey. Our minds wandered back to the uncomfortable scenario of being spiritually placed in the belly of the fish. We had been disobedient and disregarded the Lord's directions. The three of us should have learned by now that it is easier to submit in obedience the first time directions from the Lord were given. Learning from that experience, all of us agreed that faithfulness and discipline would abundantly bless the Lord. This will be a never ending goal for each of our "todays."

"Today And Forever"

> *I will instruct you and teach you in the way you should go; I will counsel you and watch over you.*
> *Psalm 32:8 (NIV)*

TODAY IS YOUR DAY OF HOPE AND TIME TO GO ON TO YOUR NEW JOURNEY

> *There is surely a future hope for you, and your hope will not be cut off. Proverbs 23:18 (NIV)*

As we came to the end of another assignment on our walk, our last four days of this particular assignment were rather painful. Thinking back on our prior positive intentions, and ultimate negative reactions, we remembered the times that we had disappointed God and those around us. Like many of you reading this right now, we rejoice with you that God is the Maker, Mediator and Master of our enemies. He is a God of Peace. He is King Jesus, Son of the Living God. When we work with God, there is nothing that we can do that can destroy our peace. No one can hurt you without your consent. We must take responsibility for our lives. Don't be controlled by the conditions you have experienced. We have the ability to choose. We should not let the people and situations of the past determine our future. Make your failures be the foundation for the success of your future. *Remember. When we are down to nothing, we can rest assured that God is up to something.* Refuse to be intimidated by your past circumstances. Giving love requires a change of character without expecting love to return to you. Some can absorb love, but are uncertain about how to give love. Don't look for ways to offend. Look for ways to keep the door of love open to all. Don't let your past define the quality of your new life. Your thoughts determine your destiny.

> *In view of this, make every effort to respond to God's promises. Supplement your faith with a generous provision of moral excellence, and moral excellence with knowledge, and knowledge with self-control, and self-control with patient endurance, and patient endurance with godliness, and godliness with brotherly affection, and brotherly affection with love for everyone.*
> 2 Peter 1:5-7 (NLT).

All three of us were in agreement that if any goal rang true on our journey, this would be the highlight and ultimate message that would enable us to move forward. The Lord was commanding us to give love as He gives divine love to all creation. We struggled with that concept. Now we will fervently strive for unspeakable joy that gives hope and peace to the "new creation" of being the people that God wants us to be. This is a goal that each of us could work to achieve. Slight bumps in the road will occur along the way, but we have the assurance that "If God is for us, who can be against us?" *WHAT A CONCEPT.*

August 8 – **"My children, these are My words"**

"Today And Forever"

"You have learned these past months what part each of you have played in these journeys. There are visions, scripture interpretations, words, and decisions that have to be made. I have been, and always will be with you, but the time has come for you to put all of My works, words, and guidance into place.

"I will come to you in prayer when you are settled and can hear Me. I will guide you into the scriptures for each challenge you will face. You must take charge, without pride, or making your own choices.

"Your visions will come much stronger. You need to be ready to listen and watch for them. The interpretations will come right along with the visions. You will be shown the outcome of the right and wrong choices when they are made. You are never to become nervous for having received them. They are needed to move forward.

"Remember, the words have to be of Me and not someone else, or the enemy. Your minds have to be clear and settled into My realm. I speak to those who listen and take My directions.

"Remember Abraham, he was the first one to believe. He did as I asked. He took his only loving son of his heart, and took him up the mountain. He was willing to give him up.

"Noah was willing to build because I said to do it. It didn't matter what anyone else told him... he did it.

"Daniel prayed and no matter what anyone else told him, he kept My commandments. He did as he was supposed to do, without any questions.

"Paul had to be changed. He did awful things, but I really got to him good.

"Peter was stoned, jailed, and almost put to death. He knew he still had to stand up for Me.

"The three of you must do your best, and do what you know I need you to do. It will be done without questions.

"The challenges and choices will be given, but you have to pick one that is according to My will. The visions and results will explain right from wrong.

"You have been on this past journey because of the challenges and choices you will have to face in the future.

"The challenges and choices are as follows, but not in any specific order.

"Your families will have challenges, but you will have choices of how to handle it. A choice must be made.

"There will be those who will need to hear about your journey. It will be a challenge, but the choices of whom to speak with will have to be there.

"Your prayer ministry will change, and it will be stronger. A challenge of where and to whom will have to be addressed.

"There will be people who will need counsel, which is always a challenge. It is important that correct choices are made, which will also include those who do not know Me.

"Others have Goliath stones, which need to be cast aside. Choices of those to whom you will speak will be part of your challenges.

"A choice of the church you are to attend will be made. The challenge will be there and choices will be given, but the right one is up to you.

"Children, I know this is quite a task I am sending you on, but I would not be giving it to you if I didn't believe you were ready. I have groomed you, prepared you, listened to you in each circumstance and still I know you can do this. It will be much harder than all the other tasks you have been assigned, but I know with My help and your learning, you will get through this one, too.

"The challenges are there. The choices are up to you. Please, My dear ones, pray hard, pray quietly, take more time for Me, no matter what the circumstances are in your lives now. It is important to Me, so therefore, it should be important to you.

"I will be giving you words, scriptures and visions continually, to start you off. I will not be the one to make the choices for you. That will be of your own accord. I have set your paths straight, so do not go off the path. You know what will happen if you do! Do not eat of the rotten fruit, or listen to the wrong voice. Keep clean, keep clear of what is thrown in your path that is not of Me. Listen, watch, and be careful. You have been without Me (without My covering), but never again. I am with you always, but you will have to make the choices of whether you will continue to hear Me.

"For now, I need you to finish the rest of these thirty day topics. When you have completed that, take time to just pray before you start the next journey. The three of you must get together to pray these last thirty days out, and get ready for the next journey.

"When the thirty days are completed, I will come again with My instructions for the next part of the journey. Get ready, listen more, and prepare more.

"For now my children, go in peace, love, gentleness, joy and self-control. I will speak with you again." Your Loving Father, God

At the beginning of our journey, there were questions about why the three of us were chosen to walk this path together. It was beyond our comprehension that God intentionally placed us together, because we came from different backgrounds and religious affiliations. Learning to trust each other and be respectful of each other's feelings and ideas was not automatic at the beginning of our journey.

When the Lord said He wanted us to go on a thirty-day journey, our reactions were mixtures of apprehension, anxiety, uneasiness, enthusiasm, and excitement. Our thoughts were, "That is not too hard. We can surely do that." Little did we know that God's timing of His thirty days was much different than our five hundred and forty-eight human calendar days (one-and-a-half years) that we had just completed. At the beginning of our journey, we didn't know about, nor understand the true fear (reverence) of the Lord. In spite of our failures, we couldn't comprehend how God could still love us enough to place us on this journey.

It was hard for us to wrap our minds around the fact that we had walked the same path together for such a time as this. We reminisced that at first we walked together as three separate people. As the journey progressed, we began to recognize that the Lord's purpose for the three of us was to bond together. Just like the strength of a three-stranded cord, we were called to be united as one.

One of the things we learned as we grew to trust and rely on each other was that God graciously extended peace and strength to at least one of us, when the other two needed prayer and encouragement.

Through all of the good times and the times we knew we had disappointed God, He consistently loved on us and challenged us to do better. He never gave up on us. We are still learning how to trust and be obedient to the Lord. Learning not to anticipate God's next move, He challenged us to "go with the flow." We might add, this was one of the most difficult lessons we experienced. Having had the personal experience of knowing the Lord does what He says He will do has been a major incentive for us to humble ourselves to listen and move without hesitation.

This journey has given the three of us the determination to continue walking the path on which the Lord has placed us. We thank God daily for allowing us to serve Him with a new awareness that we can do all things through Him who strengthens us.

We look forward with joyful anticipation to all of the "new beginnings" the Lord has in store for the three of us. It may be a roller coaster ride, but we know He will be holding our hand, walking by our side, forever!

May the grace of the Lord Jesus Christ, the love of God, and the fellowship of the Holy Spirit be with you all. 2 Corinthians 13:14 (NLT)

GOD WILL NEVER STOP BELIEVING IN YOU!

TESTIMONIES

There was so much that had happened to us, we remained in awe at every little detail of the assignments we had been given. As we allowed ourselves to race through the corridors of our memories from this journey, we recognized that God is the one that kept, and continues to keep, our world in motion, simply by speaking. We are also so grateful that He never tires of hearing the cries of our heart. We give God all of the praise, honor, and glory for allowing us to spend time with each of you, through this book.

The following three testimonies relate how this journey affected our hearts and our lives.

<u>TESTIMONY #1</u>
"With the Lord's patience, direction and gentleness, He taught me the true meaning of trust. With many medical handicaps, disappointments and struggles, trusting was never easy for me. Throughout this

journey, He saved me from times I wanted to give up and go back to a familiar place that was neither safe nor stable. It was just comfortable. In all of my laziness, mistakes and wandering, the Lord was so gracious to wait for me to come to Him. He also taught me to love and respect the opinions of others and where they are on their journey. Admitting and coming to the realization that I didn't have to be right all of the time was a humbling concept. With all His teaching, I am trying to become the person He wants me to be in mind, soul and actions. The scripture *Proverbs 3:5-8* were just words in His book until He taught me about understanding, wisdom and trust. We are never too old to learn and change. We just have to be willing to put God first."

> *Trust in the Lord with all our heart, and do not lean on your own understanding. In all ways acknowledge Him, And He will make your paths straight. Do not be wise in your own eyes; Fear the Lord and turn away from evil. It will be healing to your body, and refreshment to your bones.*
> *Proverbs 3:5-8 (NAS)*

TESTIMONY #2

"The struggles I faced throughout the journey dealt with obedience. The Lord, in His infinite wisdom, saved me from myself on more than one occasion. He lovingly (and sometimes sternly) showed me that I had a habit of 'running ahead of the Lord,' and did not wait for

His perfect timing. The Lord guided me through many trials, mistakes, and often humiliation, for the prideful actions that I displayed. I am so very grateful that by the Grace of God, He consistently loved on me and lifted me up by helping me to keep my self-worth intact. He remained patient with me until I exhibited a total awareness that obedience is about listening first, then responding the first time He asks. With God's help, I am learning to recognize my strengths and weaknesses. This prompts me to be more intentional about my obedience to the Lord in ways that will please Him. My life with the Lord is a continuous journey."

> *"Understand this, my dear brothers and sisters" You must all be quick to listen, slow to speak, and slow to get angry. Human anger does not produce the righteousness God desires. So get rid of all the filth and evil in your lives and humbly accept the word God has planted in your hearts, for it has the power to save your souls. But don't just listen to God's word. You must do what it says. Otherwise, you are only fooling yourselves. For if you listen to the word and don't obey, it is like glancing at your face in the mirror. You see yourself, walk away, and forget what you look like. But if you look carefully into the perfect law that sets you free, and if you do what it says and don't forget what you heard then God will bless you for doing it.*
> *James 1:19-25 (NLT)*

TESTIMONY #3

"Due to a physical disability that results in a continual state of discomfort, many times I was reluctant to take another step on the journey that God had called us to travel. But God quietly, and lovingly, spoke to me each of those times and reminded me of one of His scriptures that always lifted my spirit and reconnected me with His presence. Part of that scripture was, *He gives strength to the weary and increases the power of the weak.* Many days the weary was working in conjunction with the weak and discomfort, in an attempt to slow down the progress God wanted from me. All too often I was willing to set aside my part of the assignment just to relax, get some rest, and try to find some relief from the discomfort that continually plagued me. Recalling His scripture encouraged me to put aside those times, to follow His instructions. Being obedient to Him was not one of my strong points. Thanks be to God that He has been patient to lead and love me back to the realization that I belong to Him. I was created and have been called to be in service to the Living Lord. Thank You, Lord Jesus! The scripture that has encouraged and carried me through many difficult times is as follows:

> *Do you not know? Have you not heard? The Lord is the everlasting God, the Creator of the ends of the earth. He will not grow tired or weary, and his understanding no one can fathom. He gives strength to the weary and increases the power of the weak. Isaiah 40:28-29 (NIV)*

We consider it a blessing and thank each of you reading this book, for taking this journey with the three of us. As your mind wanders back over our assignments, our prayer is that you will recognize yourself on one or more of these pages. God wants each of us to realize that He loves all of His children so much, and will always be present in every area of our lives.

        BELIEVE AND RECEIVE
        THE JOY OF THE LORD

FINALLY, BROTHERS AND SISTERS

As we continue on our roller coaster journey, we still have our fifth and final stone to release. This, too, will be according to God's plan and in His perfect timing.

> *Finally, brothers and sisters, whatever is true, whatever is noble, whatever is right, whatever is pure, whatever is lovely, whatever is admirable – if anything is excellent or praiseworthy – think about such things. Whatever you have learned or received or heard from me, or seen in me – put it into practice. And the God of peace will be with you. Philippians 4:8-9 (NIV)*

CPSIA information can be obtained at www.ICGtesting.com
Printed in the USA
LVOW12s0255011014

406589LV00002B/2/P